SIDNEY REILLY

Sidney Reilly

Master Spy

BENNY MORRIS

Yale

UNIVERSITY
PRESS

New Haven and London

Jewish Lives® is a registered trademark of the Leon D. Black Foundation.

Yale University Press books may be purchased in quantity for educational,
business, or promotional use. For information, please e-mail sales.press@yale.edu
(U.S. office) or sales@yaleup.co.uk (U.K. office).

Set in Janson OldStyle type by Integrated Publishing Solutions.
Printed in the United States of America.

Library of Congress Control Number: 2021953444
ISBN 978-0-300-24826-5 (hardcover : alk. paper)

A catalogue record for this book is available from the British Library.

This paper meets the requirements of ANSI/NISO Z39.48-1992
(Permanence of Paper).

10 9 8 7 6 5 4 3 2 1

For Erel and Liat
Yagi and Omer
and Orian

CONTENTS

.

BI	Bureau of Investigation (US)
CIA	Central Intelligence Agency (US)
FO	Foreign Office (UK)
FSB	Federal Security Service (Russian Federation)
KGB	Committee for State Security (Soviet Union)
MI5	Military Intelligence 5 (UK)
MI6	Military Intelligence 6 (UK)
MO2	Military Operations 2 (UK)
MO3	Military Operations 3 (UK)
MP	Member of Parliament (UK)
RAF	Royal Air Force (UK)
RFC	Royal Flying Corps (UK)
RSC	Russian Supply Committee (US)
SIS	Secret Intelligence Service (MI6) (UK)
SR	Socialist Revolutionary Party (Russia)
SSB	Secret Service Bureau (UK)
UKNA	United Kingdom National Archives
USNA	United States National Archives
WO	War Office (UK)

SIDNEY REILLY

Introduction

"Complexion swarthy, a long straight nose, piercing eyes, black hair brushed back from a forehead suggesting keen intelligence, a large mouth, figure slight, of medium height, always clothed immaculately, he was a man that impressed one with a sense of power," was how Norman Thwaites, an officer of the Secret Intelligence Service (SIS or MI6, Britain's foreign espionage agency), described Sidney Reilly, then in his late thirties, during the First World War.

In the first half of the twentieth century, and perhaps during the second half as well, Reilly was regarded in the English-speaking world as the gold standard of espionage. Ian Fleming, the intelligence officer, playboy, and writer, once said: "James Bond is just a piece of nonsense I dreamed up. He's not a Sidney Reilly, you know." Half a dozen Reilly biographies have appeared over the years, and in 1983 Britain's Thames Television broadcast a twelve-part miniseries entitled *Reilly, Ace of Spies* devoted to his exploits, to wide acclaim and popularity. The series, in which Reilly was played by the Irish–New Zealander–British actor Sam Neill, has since been aired around the world.

Reilly became a very popular spy indeed. But he was not really a spy by profession and spent only three years of his adult life, during 1918–1921, as a full-time employee of MI6. During the rest of his adulthood, while devoting time and energy to intelligence work, espionage played second fiddle to his business ventures, which included producing and selling patent medicines and brokering arms sales and oil deals. Like James Bond, he spent much of his time womanizing and gambling, but he also collected antiques and, after 1917, lobbied, fund-raised, and organized subversion against the Bolshevik regime that had assumed power in Russia. Indeed, this became his overriding obsession and led directly to his death.

Often, Reilly, as a businessman, was accused of sharp if not actually fraudulent practices—as some put it, he was a superior con man. But through his spying and anti-Bolshevism, he transcended his pecuniary pursuits and earned himself a place in history, albeit a small one. And postmortem, he left a powerful imprint on the public imagination in the English-speaking world, and perhaps beyond, as a paragon of tradecraft.

But he was far from the perfect spy. While usually playing things close to his chest, Reilly often talked too much, especially to his women, and was prone to bragging about his exploits, even inventing some. But more generally, Reilly was simply too shifty, too money-grubbing, too insubordinate, and too dissolute—always an opening for blackmail—to fit into a modern state espionage agency. He had three or four wives (simultaneously, adulterously) and a girl in every port. As one biographer has written, "women fell to [his] irresistible charm like leaves from the trees in autumn." Yet he was "not above making love with the *Financial Times* on his pillow," according to one woman who knew him. He may have loved some of his women, but he was a cold, calculating—though never cruel—exploiter of the female sex.

He clearly possessed some of the essential attributes of a spy. He spoke at least four languages with complete fluency—Russian, English, German, and French—and he may have spoken as many as six, but all with "an accent equally foreign," as his third or fourth wife Pepita once put it. He was proficient at disguises and dissimulation. At times he passed himself off, successfully, as a Greek or Turkish merchant or a German machine-tool operator, and even as an Irishman (presumably few Russian or Estonian officials could differentiate between an Englishman, an English-speaking Turk, or an Irishman).

But Sidney Reilly was no Irishman. Indeed, he wasn't really "Sidney Reilly." It was the name his British handler, or he himself, conjured up to facilitate his operations on the Continent—and for Reilly, it was also an aid to hiding or distancing himself from his Jewish origins. Before becoming Reilly, he was Sigmund or Shlomo Rosenblum.

Nazis and, perhaps, communists would have seen in Reilly the ultimate "cosmopolitan Jew." But he was not rootless; as an adult, he had one or two very firm loyalties, above all to Great Britain. He apparently gave supreme proof of this in his last days as his Soviet captors, before executing him, proved unable to extract from him any practically useful intelligence about his fellow British agents. To the last, he called himself an Englishman. But his Jewish identity was another matter. As we trace what we can of his life, we will see him—on rare occasions—confront the "Jewish question." But more often we see him elide it or ignore it altogether, in both personal and collective contexts.

For those interested in the history of espionage, Reilly bridged the gap between the amateur and the professional spy. The governmental intelligence agencies that loomed large in the twentieth century and figure in current international affairs—KGB (FSB), CIA, MI6—were all born around the two world wars. Before 1909, intelligence departments were small offshoots of operations branches of states' armies or navies. These departments were occasionally, haphazardly, served by businessmen, explorers, archeologists, and tourists, who supplied tidbits of information. Reilly was one of these part-timers—until his induction into MI6. In general, it took decades for the upper and upper-middle classes in the West to discard the notion that spying was a tainted vocation, an ungentlemanly pursuit; decent people did not open other people's mail or peek through keyholes. And as we shall see, for most of his life the gentlemen around him regarded Reilly as a dubious, shady quantity.

One last, but necessary, word. Writing about spies is problematic, especially about ones who died a century ago. They usually operated in the shadows and then, if not caught, retired into obscurity. Those who knew them are long dead and cannot be interviewed. And the documentation about their activities, if any was produced, is usually shut away and classified, beyond the reach of the thirty-year, fifty-year, or seventy-five-year rules that generally govern the release of government papers in democracies. What is available about Reilly—in the British and American national archives, in Russia, and in several collections of private papers—I have outlined in the Bibliographical Note at the end of this book.

1

Beginnings

SIGMUND (or Shlomo or Zalman or Salomon or "little Georgie") Rosenblum—later Sidney Reilly—may have descended, through his paternal grandfather, from the eighteenth-century Grand Rabbi of Prague Ezekiel Landau, and from Elijah ben Solomon, the Gaon of Vilna. He may also have been related to Leon Trotsky, the Soviet leader. He may have been born in Odessa, Ukraine—as the Soviet authorities later determined—or in nearby Kherson, or in Russian-ruled Poland at Bendzin (near Auschwitz) or Pruzhany, on or around March 24, 1874 (though other versions have it that he came into this world in 1872).

His mother was Beila (or Paulina) Altmann (or Berenstein or Bronstein), a well-educated Jew from a middle-class Kherson or Odessa family. She may have converted to Catholicism before Reilly's birth. In or around 1870 she married Gersh Yakovlevich Rosenblum, a timber merchant. Their marriage seems to have been unhappy. Gersh may have been Sigmund's father, but it is also possible that Sidney Reilly was sired by Vladimir Rosenblum, Gersh's brother, or one Mikhail Rosenblum, a cousin of Gersh's, a medical doctor and Paulina's erstwhile lover.

During his teens in Odessa, Reilly apparently was made aware of his doubtful paternity, and according to George Hill, his friend and fellow MI6 officer, "throughout the years, he had a chip on his shoulder about being a bastard." Hill was among several MI6 investigators who during the 1920s (unsuccessfully) tried to uncover details about Reilly's origins. Reilly himself, in later life, told people that his father was an unnamed colonel in the Russian army or a Russian count or even an Irish or British sea captain, implying that he was at best (or worst) only half-Jewish, in keeping with his efforts, throughout life, to distance himself from his Jewish roots.

Paulina, as she preferred to call herself, wanted her children—Reilly and his two sisters, Mariam (or Anna) and Elena—to grow up cultured and gentile. Only German and Polish were spoken at home, not Yiddish, and the children were taught French, English, Greek, and Latin. Anna was the one Reilly remained closest to, and he kept in infrequent contact with her until her suicide in Paris around 1900. Reilly seems to have attended a Russian-speaking school and avoided *cheder*, the traditional Jewish elementary school where children learned Hebrew, prayers, Talmud, and some Bible. A sickly child, Reilly bonded with his mother. With his father, Gersh, he enjoyed only a distant relationship; Gersh seems often to have been away on business.

When Reilly was in his teens, a dispute broke out between Gersh and his brother Vladimir (whether over business or personal matters, or both, is unclear) and, immediately after, Paulina left her husband, taking Reilly and Elena to Odessa. They lived at 15 Aleksandrovskii Prospect and Reilly attended Gymnasia (high school) No. 3. He may have gone on from there, as he later told people, to study physics and mathematics at Odessa

University or chemistry at the University of Vienna, though neither school's records contain reference to him. Perhaps he merely audited classes; perhaps he just made it all up.

But he clearly spent part of his youth, and perhaps childhood as well, in Odessa, which in a number of ways equipped him for and shaped his adulthood. Born there or not, Reilly was very much an Odessan Jew. There, he learned the ways of the world and its prominent languages, and made friends and contacts who periodically would crop up in the course of his life.

At the southern end of the Pale of Settlement—the area allowed for Jewish habitation in the tsarist empire—Odessa, toward the end of the nineteenth century, was a special place, European, cosmopolitan, modern. Three thousand years before, Greeks had settled the Black Sea littoral and its encroaching hilltops. During Ottoman days, a small town, Khazhibei, emerged where the Dniester River poured into the sea. Beside it the sultans built a fort, Yeni Dunya. When, at the end of the eighteenth century, the armies of Catherine the Great, the empress of Russia, conquered the area, her Neapolitan mercenary, Admiral José de Ribas, designated the location suitable for a port that would serve as the gateway to southern Russia. Construction of a modern city began in 1794 and Khazhibei was renamed Odessa (after the ancient Greek colony of Odessos, which was believed to have existed in the area). There would be symmetrical streets, broad tree-lined avenues, and an up-to-date harbor. Another European, the exiled French duke Armand de Richelieu, employed as prefect by Catherine's descendant Alexander I, modernized the municipal administration, planted parks, and built impressive public structures, including a theater and library. Richelieu's statue at the head of the monumental staircase—the one that figures large in Serge Eisenstein's film *Battleship Potemkin*—remains one of the city's landmarks.

Both de Ribas and Richelieu were friendly and tolerant toward Odessa's Jews and, in an effort to increase its international trade, encouraged Jews from other parts of the empire, especially from Galicia, to settle in the town. Jewish numbers swelled and trade flourished, though this gave rise to hostility by the competing Greek community. By the mid-nineteenth century, the town had a "Continental appearance . . . 'full of affluence, movement, and gaiety,'" in the words of historian Steven Zipperstein. Goods poured through the port—grain from Ukraine and southern Russia, spices from the east, cloth and industrial products from the Continent. Thousands of nonresident foreigners—sailors, merchants, soldiers, and tourists—inundated its cafes, shops, and harbor.

"In Odessa, you can smell Europe," the Russian poet Pushkin once wrote. Like Istanbul, Odessa, at once a frontier town and maritime crossroads, mixed Europe and Asia, high culture and rowdiness. Odessa had a prominent criminal underbelly, about which Isaac Babel famously wrote. Its shanty neighborhoods were packed with the poor, smugglers, pickpockets, thieves, and lowlifes of every type, Jews among them. Ze'ev (Vladimir) Jabotinsky, the right-wing Zionist leader, who hailed from Odessa, once described the archetypal Odessan as "experienced, shrewd, a trickster, a manipulator, a maneuverer, a man of ingenuity, a screamer, an exaggerator [and] a speculator." Most of these adjectives were later applied to Sidney Reilly.

By 1890 Odessa had some 400,000 inhabitants, most of them Christian Russians and Ukrainians, with a smattering of Tatars, Cossacks, Moldovans, Greeks, Italians, Germans, Armenians, and even Karaites. A full one-quarter to one-third of the population—and much of its middle class—was Jewish. Jews figured prominently in the city's schools, culture, and economic life (two-thirds of its industries, workshops, and commercial companies were Jewish-owned). Dostoyevsky was to refer to Odessa as "the city of Yids." Among Odessa's most famous sons were Leon Trotsky (né Lev Bronstein, born in a village near Kherson but raised in Odessa), the writer Babel, the Nobel Prize–

winning zoologist and immunologist Elie Mechnikov, and the violinist David Oistrakh.

By contrast with most of Russia, the city had a reputation as tolerant and welcoming. The town's cosmopolitan atmosphere had a secularizing and liberalizing effect on Odessa's Jewish community. One observer in the 1880s noted that almost all the Jewish shops remained open for business on the Sabbath, and increasingly Odessa's Jews—especially of the middle class—spoke Russian. But the anti-Semitism that pervaded Russia during the late nineteenth century did not pass Odessa by. The year 1871 witnessed a four-day pogrom, in which dozens of Jews were murdered or injured and hundreds of Jewish homes and shops were damaged or destroyed; thousands became homeless. The Odessa pogrom was triggered by a rumor that Jews had desecrated the Greek Orthodox church, but in the background was a sense that the town's Jews were growing too wealthy and economically dominant. There were further pogroms in 1881 and 1905. Around the fin de siècle, Odessa Jewish community leaders noted that, growingly, headmasters in state schools were refusing admission to Jewish applicants and teachers were taunting Jewish pupils.

In 1893, the young Reilly was arrested by the Okhrana, the tsarist secret police, perhaps after returning from Vienna, and spent a week in solitary confinement in a windowless cell. The authorities suspected him of involvement in (an innocuous) socialist student group called the League of Enlightenment—though it seems to have been a superficial youthful involvement, with no depth; in later years he was to display no sympathy for the revolutionary cause (though he did consistently reject tsardom). Upon his release from jail he learned that his mother had died. At the preinterment family gathering, one of his uncles chided him: "What can you expect from a dirty little Jewish bastard!" Perhaps the uncle was hinting at the paternity of Dr. Mikhail Rosenblum, his mother's lover.

This personal slight appears to have hit the young man front and center, coming on top of the imprisonment and his mother's sudden death. There was nothing, it seemed, to keep him in Odessa. A day or two after the funeral, Reilly fled the country. At a stroke, he left behind the entanglement with the Okhrana (who may even have tried to recruit him to spy on his fellow students—revolutionaries turned tsarist secret police informers during the waning years of the Empire were common; Joseph Stalin, the future Communist leader, was certainly one) and his first cousin Felicia, the daughter of Vladimir, with whom he apparently had fallen in love. Earlier, he may have hoped to marry her, but on both sides, the family opposed the match. Although Reilly left Odessa, he was to retain a lifelong affection for Felicia, and they were in sporadic contact over the years. (She died in Auschwitz during World War Two, almost two decades after he himself had passed.)

Reilly was now a nineteen- or twenty-year-old, alone in the world and penniless. He had permanently—as it turned out—cut himself loose from his origins and family. He had to live by his wits and fend for himself; there was no safety net. It is not clear what Reilly did during the following two years. He may have washed up in Brazil, as he was later to claim, possibly working there, or elsewhere, as a cook, boatman, and dockhand; and he may, as he also later claimed, have caught the eye of British intelligence officers traveling in South America. What is certain is that by late 1895 he was back in Europe. In the interim, he may have briefly taken or at least started to take courses in metallurgy or chemistry (or even philosophy) in Germany or Switzerland, though no trace of his presence has been found in the registries of central Europe's universities during 1893–1895.

By late 1895, Reilly was living in Paris. How he subsisted is unknown, but he probably made some money by serving as an informant for the Okhrana's Western European spymaster, the Paris-based Petr Ivanovich Rachkovskii. Rachkovskii kept tabs on the city's large and in great part anti-tsarist Russian émigré community, which at times included Lenin (who called Paris "a foul hole"—he preferred Berlin) and Trotsky.

Reilly's connection with the Okhrana may have started in his last months in Odessa—or it may have been something completely new, albeit with an "Odessan" link. One of the Okhrana's main operatives in Paris was Ivan Fedorovich Manasevich-Manuilov, a young Jew who worked as a correspondent for *Novosti*, a Russian-language newspaper. One of Manasevich's agents was Boris Nadel—and Nadel was a friend of Reilly's from Odessa. It was probably Nadel who brought Reilly and Manasevich together, whereupon Reilly was hired to snoop on the city's Russian émigrés. We don't know whether he received a retainer or did piecework, but there was certainly money to be made.

On December 25, 1895, perhaps on assignment from Manasevich, Reilly and a colleague (possibly a penurious journalist named Alexander Matzebovich) attacked and robbed two anarchist couriers carrying cash on a train between Paris and Fontainebleau, killing one and mortally wounding the other. One of the victims, Constant della Cassa, an Italian, according to a contemporary newspaper report was found "lying unconscious in the middle of a pool of blood. His throat had been cut and his body bore the marks of numerous knife wounds." French police looked for the killers. Reilly's hasty departure for London that week may indicate guilt—or it may just have been a coincidence. In any event, he arrived in the British capital via a cross-Channel ferry before year's end. He also came to what would be his new homeland with a great deal of cash (as much as $75,000 in current values), as evidenced by his spending spree during the following days.

Reilly took rooms in a house in South Lambeth, bought fancy clothes, made friends with fellow Russian émigrés (on the orders of the Okhrana?), and embarked on three parallel careers, all of which he was to pursue, simultaneously or in staggered fashion, until his death three decades later: businessman, con man, and spy. Perhaps one should add to this a fourth career, as a ladies' man, which henceforth was to take up much of his time and energy.

He began appraising, buying, and selling objets d'art for Wilfrid Michael Voynich, a Russian married to Ethel Lillian Boole Voynich, an Irish-born novelist and the daughter of the famed mathematician and philosopher George Boole. It is likely that Ethel and Reilly became lovers. In 1897 she published a novel, *The Gadfly*, whose adventurer hero, Arthur Burton, shared traits with Reilly. He also began to collect objets d'art, over the following years building up a valuable collection of Napoleonica. He appears to have had an eye for good art and antiques.

The art market was Reilly's entrée into the business world. But more important to his unfolding dealings was the fellowship he managed to wangle in Britain's Chemical Society, with a parallel membership in the Institute of Chemistry. He also received a reader's card at the British Museum, describing himself in his application as "a chemist and physicist and a member of various scientific institutions." These affiliations helped him land a job as a consultant in the Electric Ozone Company, which produced chemicals and ozone generators for purifying water and air. Reilly was nothing if not enterprising. He soon met the Greek arms dealer and shipbuilding magnate Basil Zaharoff. Zaharoff was to become, as one Reilly biographer put it, "Reilly's most significant role model." Reilly at this time set up two patent medicine companies, Rosenblum & Company and the Ozone Preparations Company, producing and selling dubious medicinal concoctions (among them "Tibetan remedies" and, as a Reilly biographer put it, "sundry panaceas compounded of herbs, alcohol, a dash of opiates here, and pinches of Cocaine there"). It was the age of the patent medicine racket and miracle cures, and Reilly was on top of it.

But it was not all business. Within months, Reilly resumed his espionage activities, initially for the Okhrana, where he was code-named *Khimik* (the Chemist), and then for Scotland Yard's Special Branch, which collaborated with the Paris office of the Okhrana in keeping tabs on Western Europe's Russian émigré communities and here and there arrested revolutionaries and anarchists.

The man who ran these operations in London was the Catholic Irish-born Scotland Yard superintendent William Melville, who in 1893 took over the headship of the Yard's Special Branch. Founded in 1887, the Special Branch replaced the Yard's Special Irish Branch, where Melville, after starting adult life as a baker, had begun his career monitoring Irish revolutionaries. He went on to specialize in the political émigré communities, seen at the time as the seedbed of anarchism. In 1892 he "uncovered" a band of anarchists in what became known as the Walsall Plot, apparently a provocation he himself had stage-managed. Curiously, Melville's son, James Melville, a barrister, defended leading anarchists (including Jacob Peters—or Jekabs Peterss—the future Bolshevik secret police executive), and eventually became a Labour Party MP and England's solicitor general.

The anarchists, some of whom in the 1880s and 1890s turned to terrorism (they called it "propaganda of the deed"), opposed the modern state and wanted societies without government, law, or private ownership, to be run as voluntary associations. It was, as one historian put it, "a daydream of desperate romantics." They especially hated authoritarian regimes, though they managed to commit outrages that primarily killed democratic leaders (perhaps because dictators, better guarded, were more difficult to target). In November 1893 anarchists blew up Barcelona's Liceu opera house, killing and seriously wounding dozens of the city's elite, and they went on to murder President Sadi Carnot of France (June 1894), Spanish prime minister Antonio Canovas del Castillo (August 1897), Empress Elisabeth of

Austria (September 1898), King Umberto I of Italy (July 1900), and US president William McKinley (September 1901), among many others. In London in the 1890s, revolutionary anarchists were considered a mortal threat to the West's order and stability, much as Muslim extremists were seen at the start of the twenty-first century. In the 1890s, some European officials believed that there was a vast, continent-encompassing anarchist conspiracy behind the spate of assassinations—though in fact, there were simply like-minded cells of terroristic anarchists in different countries doing their thing without coordination.

Reilly signed on with Melville in 1896. Melville may have initially taken him on because of Reilly's in with the Voynich couple: Wilfrid moved in London's anti-tsarist émigré circles, a target of the Okhrana. By then, Melville had established a good working relationship with the Paris-based Rachkovskii, the head of the Okhrana's foreign operations, who frequently visited London accompanied by a batch of officers in mufti. Melville described Rachkovskii as "a very hospitable man and of genial character," but didn't really trust him. Unbeknownst to Melville, Rachkovskii was probably responsible for the fabrication of *The Protocols of the Elders of Zion*, the infamous anti-Semitic tract.

Aside from looking at émigré groups in London, Melville at this time also seems to have overseen espionage operations, authorized by Britain's Naval Intelligence Department, against Germany, which was believed to be building a counterweight to Britain's Royal Navy. In the years around the turn of the century, Melville apparently sent Reilly to Germany, perhaps a number of times, to gather intelligence on naval construction and armaments development.

Despite occasional friction with the two rival imperial powers, France and Russia, many Britons at this time growingly saw Germany as Britain's primary potential enemy. The fear of Germany focused on its efficient land army (which had easily bested France in the Franco-Prussian War of 1870) and on German naval construction, which threatened to challenge Britain's mastery of the seas. Some Britons feared that a combination of German naval and ground units posed a real threat to Britain itself, and that hosts of German spies were busy gathering information about possible landing sites on England's coastline and British defensive capabilities. The spy fever was pumped up by such writers as Erskine Childers, E. Phillips Oppenheim, and William Le Queux, with the latter's *Spies of the Kaiser* (1909) and *The Invasion of 1910* (1906) serialized in Lord Northcliffe's popular *Daily Mail*. Melville later credited Le Queux with "waking up the public" to the German threat.

Reilly probably earned very little money from his spying chores for Melville. But having seen how the rich lived in London and Paris, he set his mind on ascending the socioeconomic ladder. And then along came a (relatively) big fish: the Welsh reverend Hugh Thomas, a wealthy horse breeder (Reilly, forever the gambler, also had an interest in horses). The sixty-five-year-old Thomas had recently married Margaret Callahan, a twenty-three-year-old Irish woman, who may have been his nurse or household servant. She was born in the village of Courtown Harbour, County Wexford, in 1874.

Reilly met and befriended the couple in late 1897 or early 1898, it is unclear where or how. Perhaps it was at a racetrack or through the sale of objets d'art, with which Thomas filled his two houses, in London and Wales. Or—somewhat less likely—it could have been in Russia, where Reilly was sent by Melville on a mission and the Thomases were touring. Whatever the case, Reilly soon discovered that Thomas had a small fortune in cash and stocks. And that he had a weak heart and was often housebound. Margaret soon tired of her infirm husband. Reilly, on the other hand, was young, attractive, and vigorous, and very ambitious. Margaret fell hard. Perhaps Reilly, too, was genuinely smitten. He may have seduced her (he called her Margaritka, "Daisy" in Russian)—or perhaps it was the other way round. (In the 1980s Thames TV series *Reilly, Ace of Spies*, Margaret appears as an attractive middle-class lady.)

In early 1898 Margaret announced that she was pregnant and the Thomases decided to vacation in France. On March 4, 1898, Thomas made out a new will, leaving all—reportedly £10,000–12,000, apart from real estate—to Margaret. Nine days later, in Newhaven en route to Paris, with Margaret at his side, Thomas was dead. It is possible that his heart simply gave out, but poisoning, by his wife and the new family friend, seems more likely. The death certificate—signed by one Dr. S. (or T.) W. Andrews, a physician researchers have been unable to trace—noted "Morbus Cordis Syncope" (heart failure), thus precluding an inquest, and Margaret hastily arranged a burial in Llansadwrn, Anglesey, far from Newhaven. A decade later, in 1908, one Louisa Lewis, whose father had owned Newhaven's London & Paris Hotel, where Thomas had expired, disappeared from her room in London's Cecil Hotel where she had worked. She had met "Dr. T. W. Andrews" in Newhaven the morning Thomas had died; perhaps she had accidentally encountered this same man ten years later in the lobby of the Cecil—where Reilly was staying at the time—and recognized Reilly/"Andrews." If so, she clearly had to disappear. Her body was never found.

The police failed to investigate Thomas's death, and five months later, on August 22, 1898, after Margaret had had an abortion, Sigmund Georgevich Rosenblum, twenty-five, and Margaret, twenty-four, daughter of Edward Reilly Callahan, were married in the Register Office in Holborn, London. They then honeymooned in Ostend and Brussels. Later in life, the Catholic Margaret said she was "damned." The abortion—and the murder?—likely blighted their relations. But no doubt, the marriage was also eroded by Reilly's unrestrained gambling, which ate through Margaret's inheritance, and his frequent away-time with prostitutes and chorus girls—though he may have been seeking among them not just a good time, but information required by Melville about other habitués of the demimonde.

By 1899, Reilly was ready to extend his business dealings and his spying beyond Britain's shores. A change of name was called for. It was certainly easier to travel and do business abroad, particularly in Russia, with the name Reilly rather than Rosenblum. Besides, Reilly wanted to cast off any last vestige of his Jewish roots. On June 2, the Foreign Office issued him a passport in the name of Reilly—though it was only several years later, in 1908, that he formally changed his name after appealing to the High Court in London. In that appeal he stated that he had adopted the name Sidney George Reilly back in 1899 but that the deed poll he had submitted then had been "lost or destroyed."

Where had the new name come from? Most likely from Melville, his Special Branch handler. Melville's first wife Catherine's maiden name had been Reilly. Another possibility was through Margaret's father, who had appeared in the Rosenblum-Thomas marriage certificate with the middle name Reilly. But this may have been a fake name, added to Callahan on Melville's advice. Later, to reinforce the Reilly moniker, the spy would claim that he had been born in the village of Clonmel in Tipperary, Ireland. In something of an in-joke, Reilly reportedly told a friend years later that Odessa, where some people were alleging that he had been born, was "a long, long way from Tipperary."

In 1899 Reilly's business career appeared to be going nowhere: his patent medicine ventures were faltering and he was short of cash. Moreover, he had been caught out associating with a gang of Russian émigrés forging Russian banknotes—and the Russian government was about to send to England a team of investigators, who had asked for Melville's assistance. Special Branch may have felt in a bind, given that Reilly was one of theirs. Lastly, Margaret appears to have taken to drink and was perpetually on edge. For Reilly, going abroad may have appeared a good solution. One can assume that his departure was at least in part at the behest of British intelligence and Melville, who may have "loaned" him to the Admiralty's Naval Intelligence Department with a specific purpose in mind. Reilly soon surfaced in the Far East.

2

Reilly Spreads His Wings

REILLY HAD DONE his internship with the Okhrana in Paris (and perhaps before that, in Odessa) and under Melville in London. Now, around 1900, he joined the global great game of espionage, between states. During the following years he was to serve a number of masters, while giving the British pride of place—and eventually, as we shall see, exclusivity over his services (though in his final years he acted against the Communist regime in Russia out of personal compulsion and ideological commitment rather than on orders from London). At the same time, from 1900 on, until 1925, the year of his death, making money seems to have remained Reilly's overriding priority, with espionage, whatever its target or orchestration, running a mere second. Indeed, some of his espionage activities appeared, from his perspective, geared primarily to money-making. And of course, there was always sex. His sojourns outside Britain often involved meeting or accumulating lovers, his seductions and conquests no doubt facilitated by the aura of mystery surrounding his persona and by the obvious wealth he had accumulated, as generated by his various activities. According to Robin Lockhart, one of his biographers, Reilly had an "irresistible charm."

Reilly's whereabouts during 1900–1901 are unclear. He may have spent much of the time in England or, alternatively, in the Far East. Or he may have been on a succession of missions for the British War Office or the Naval Intelligence Department in Germany, Spain, and Holland. He later told friends or hinted that he had stolen German arms production secrets or aided the British cause during the Boer War by preventing Dutch or German armaments from reaching the Boers. And he certainly spent time in Paris, where he had an affair with French actress Ève Lavallière, of the Théâtre des Variétés in Montmartre. He also appears to have spent time in European Russia and in Baku, Azerbaijan, where oil was just being discovered.

His handler was most likely still Melville, who in 1903 had moved from the police to the War Office's Directorate of Military Operations. The directorate that year set up two embryonic intelligence sections, MO2 and MO3, respectively charged with foreign intelligence and counterintelligence at home. Melville appears to have been "chief investigator" for both sections. During his years with MO2 and MO3, Melville sent officers abroad on specific missions. For example, in 1904 we know that he dispatched his assistant, Herbert Dale Long, to Germany, under commercial cover, to probe local naval construction. Melville continued working for British intelligence during the following decade and a half. He was among the officers transferred by the directorate to the Secret Service Bureau, established in the summer of 1909 and jointly led by Vernon Kell (responsible for counterintelligence) and Mansfield Cumming ("C," responsible for foreign intelligence). In 1910, the SSB formally split into two organizations—the Security

Service, soon to be called MI5, and the Secret Intelligence Service, soon to be called MI6, respectively under Kell and Cumming. Melville served both branches per need and case during the following years, until his death in 1918.

By 1901, Melville's man Reilly had surfaced in the Far East. He had probably decided to go to Port Arthur for personal, commercial reasons—but had agreed, on the side, to supply British intelligence with information. Port Arthur, at the tip of the Liaotung Peninsula in Manchuria, was the Russian Pacific fleet's home base, and without doubt Britain, especially the Admiralty, was interested in what was brewing along the Pacific rim, where the expansionist empires of Russia and Japan were vying for supremacy. The two main regional prizes were Korea and Manchuria, with vast China running a vaguer, larger third. In all three, raw materials and commercial advantage were at stake. Britain had a direct interest in the outcome. In January 1902, Britain signed an agreement with Japan geared to securing their mutual interests in Manchuria. The agreement implicitly pointed at Russia as their joint "problem."

In 1900 or 1901 Reilly had met a Danish businessman, Captain Hans Nils Andersen, who headed the East Asiatic Company. The company was based in Copenhagen and had a subsidiary, the Russian East Asiatic Steamship Company (RVAPO). Reilly may have been introduced to Andersen by Moisei Akimovich Ginsburg, an old friend from Odessa. Ginsburg was a major figure in Odessa's Jewish community and a businessman with large Far Eastern commercial interests. Andersen, taken with Reilly, offered him work in the RVAPO Port Arthur branch, and Reilly and Margaret set off—either by rail, across Siberia, or by boat via Egypt and Shanghai—arriving in Port Arthur in 1901. Ginsburg was waiting for him on the pier. In addition to his duties for RVAPO, Reilly was installed by Ginsburg as an executive officer in his own Ginsburg & Company and in its subsidiary organization, the Russo-Chinese Timber Company, which provided the Russian forces on the Pacific with wood, foodstuffs, cement, and other provisions. Ginsburg & Company in Port Arthur also represented a number of Japanese companies. Duke Kirill Vladimirovich, a senior Russian naval officer who, in 1925, was to proclaim himself the successor to the assassinated Tsar Nicholas II and Russia's emperor in exile, later wrote that Ginsburg was a "benefactor on whom the entire [Russian] Pacific navy depended. . . . Everything—from a pin to an anchor, and from rivets to a smoke stack—we got everything from Ginsburg." By 1904, Reilly apparently ran all of Ginsburg's Port Arthur operations.

Before setting off for the Far East, Reilly may also have met (though this is speculative), in either Paris or St. Petersburg, Colonel Akashi Motojiro, the director of Japanese espionage in Europe. Formally, Akashi was Japanese military attaché successively in France (1901), Russia (1902), and Stockholm (1904), and during 1904–1905 is known to have run Japanese intelligence in Europe, focusing on countering the Russians. Akashi had extensive ties with anti-tsarist émigrés like Koni Zilliacus (later a prominent British Labour Party member of parliament) and financed their subversive operations against Moscow. Akashi also closely monitored Okhrana operations, including those of Ivan Manasevich-Manuilov. Akashi believed that "the best spies were those who worked for hard cash." Reilly could not have agreed more. Quite possibly Akashi recruited the "Irishman" in Europe. (Akashi went on to have a notable career. He received the Third Order of the Golden Kite for his services, was promoted to lieutenant general, and served as Japan's governor of Taiwan.)

How much spying Reilly actually did in Port Arthur, and for whom, remains moot. He was later said to have spied there either for the British, the Russians, or the Japanese, or for any combination of these. Due to his commercial activities and contacts, Reilly was well placed to gather information on the Russian deployment in Port Arthur and on their supply chains and stockpiles.

It has been suggested in previous Reilly biographies that intelligence transmitted by him to Tokyo substantially aided the Japanese in planning and executing their (relatively) successful surprise attack on the night of February 8, 1904, on the Russian fleet in Port Arthur (an attack that in some ways prefigured the Japanese assault on the American Pacific Fleet in December 1941). The attacking flotilla of Japanese destroyers penetrated the Russian port defenses—avoiding the shore batteries, most of which were nonoperational—and, using torpedoes, managed to severely damage several Russian battleships. The engagement, and a battle at sea outside the harbor between the fleets the following day, proved indecisive, but the Russians suffered greater casualties and damage.

Russian intelligence later concluded that the Japanese had received intelligence about the port defenses—but not from Reilly. They identified a Chinese engineer, Ho Liang Shung, as Japan's helper. In any event, the intelligence, whatever its source, did little to aid the Japanese in their siege of Port Arthur that followed the naval strike, or in their eventual conquest of the town in the summer of 1905. Indeed, according to a leading historian of the battle, "The Japanese army possessed relatively little hard intelligence about the strength of Russian fortifications at Port Arthur. . . . [The Japanese commander later] acknowledged that they [had] lacked adequate intelligence."

Reilly's sojourn in Port Arthur had a decisive personal dimension, however. Months after arriving in the town Reilly packed off Margaret, by then addicted to alcohol and perhaps opium, to a hospital in Belgium—and then took up with another woman, named Anne, who may also have been employed in Ginsburg & Company. It is possible that this was none other than Anne Luke, who had figured in a court case in Yokohama, Japan, in 1896 following the death by poisoning of one Walter

Carew, a businessman and her former lover. Carew's wife, Edith, was convicted of the murder by a British consular court and sentenced to death, though the sentence was later commuted to life imprisonment. At the trial, Edith had accused Anne of being the killer.

Sometime in late 1903 or early 1904, Reilly and Anne left for Japan as the Japanese forces closed in on Port Arthur. He later said that she was the only woman he ever loved. One writer has suggested that Anne bore him a son, and it is possible that he actually married her. Although Anne quickly disappeared from the Reilly story, as, successively, did almost all the other women with whom he was involved, a decade or so later, when he joined the Royal Flying Corps in Canada (later the Royal Air Force), Reilly named his next of kin as Mrs. A. Reilly, with an address in New York City.

Whatever Reilly's relations with the shadowy Anne, they failed to interfere with his other pursuits. There is firm evidence that soon after leaving Port Arthur, Reilly took up with yet another woman, Irene Harlow Dawson (née Gates), probably in Shanghai. In his April 1905 petition to divorce Irene, Frederic William Dawson named Sidney George Reilly as his "co-respondent." Frederic, a peripatetic businessman originally from Yorkshire, and Irene, an American "who represented herself to be wealthy," were married in Holy Trinity Cathedral in Shanghai in May 1903. But the marriage, according to Frederic's court petition, proved "singularly unhappy" and the two quickly separated. Later that year, Reilly and Irene "cohabited as man and wife" and "frequently committed adultery" on board the steamship *Tremont* plying its way toward Manila. Then in March–April 1904, Reilly and Irene again "cohabited as man and wife"—registering as "Mr. and Mrs. Gray"—at the Intercontinental Hotel in Rio de Janeiro, where they again "frequently committed adultery." The two subsequently went their separate ways, and then, short of cash, Irene sued Mr. Dawson for the "restitution of conjugal rights"—that is, she wanted to resurrect her marriage or perhaps lay hold of some of Dawson's assets. But Dawson, who had learned of his wife's affair with Reilly shortly after marrying her, instead petitioned for divorce in Johannesburg, South Africa; it was finally granted in 1907.

By 1905, Reilly was back in Paris, telling friends about his biggest coup, later known as the "D'Arcy Affair." The story probably contained more than an ounce of truth.

Reilly, it seems, had begun to take an interest in Persian oil exploration before reaching Port Arthur, and may well have accompanied oil explorers prospecting in northern Persia either before or during his stay in Manchuria. By 1904, the British Admiralty was beginning seriously to consider converting from coal to oil to fuel its world-spanning fleets. Such a conversion would vastly increase the ships' range, obviating the need for continuously stopping and filling up at coaling stations. It also required securing oil resources.

Three years before, in 1901, an Australian financier named William Knox D'Arcy, who had made his fortune in gold, secured from the Shah of Iran, for £10,000, an exclusive sixty-year concession to exploit oil in most of his territory. But D'Arcy needed financing, both to explore and, eventually, to extract. He turned to the French branch of the Rothschilds. Whitehall got wind of this—and sought to persuade D'Arcy to opt for financing by a British bank, so as to assure the concession for Britain. As Reilly later related, the crucial D'Arcy-Rothschild meeting was to take place aboard the Rothschild yacht docked in Cannes. Reilly, so the story went, managed to board the boat disguised as a priest, buttonholed D'Arcy, and somehow convinced him to forgo the Rothschild offer and sign on with British companies. An alternative version of the story has Reilly, again dressed as a priest, board an American vessel and prevent D'Arcy from reaching a deal with an American company, Standard Oil, owned by John D. Rockefeller. A third version, the least likely, has Reilly, sent by Melville to vacation on the Côte d'Azur, producing a (fake) written report dismissing the feasibility of the exploratory Persian drilling and getting it into the Rothschilds' hands, inducing them to back out of signing on with D'Arcy.

Whatever the case, in May 1905 the British company Burmah Oil agreed to back D'Arcy's concession, eventually setting up the Anglo-Persian Oil Company, a large share of which was owned by the Admiralty. Three years later, oil indeed was struck in Persia, and D'Arcy, and Anglo-Persian Oil (in 1954 renamed British Petroleum [BP]), reaped the reward and the Admiralty had its fuel. In the course of World War One, under First Lord of the Admiralty Winston Churchill, the Royal Navy gradually switched from coal to oil, the first of the world's major navies to do so.

In October 1905, Reilly resurfaced in St. Petersburg, accompanying Manasevich, who had been recalled by the Okhrana from Paris. The Russians and Japanese had just signed the Treaty of Portsmouth (September 1905) ending their war, and in Russia the Revolution of 1905—triggered indirectly by that war—was winding down. The tsar, Nicholas II, was reasserting control.

Reilly arrived in town posing as a British businessman, in Russian records appearing as Sidnei Georg'evich Raille. Presenting himself as a Freemason, he gained entry into Russian financial and intellectual circles, where freemasonry was rampant (the future Russian revolutionary prime minister Alexander Kerensky was a Freemason, and both Lenin and Trotsky were said to have been). Reilly joined St. Petersburg's Astrea Lodge, many of whose members were liberals and anti-tsarist.

Like many Europeans around the fin de siècle, Reilly was an aviation enthusiast; flight was the future and pilots were seen as the pioneers of a new age. Reilly also appreciated the money-making potential of aviation, military and civilian, and often attended European air shows. Once in Russia, he joined the Imperial All-Russian Aero Club (IVAK). In 1909, Reilly and two friends, Boris Souvorin and Alexander Grammatikoff, set up a company that would import French aircraft and run a flight school in St. Petersburg. In 1910 the three helped organize a flying club, the Wings Aviation Club, and staged a 390-mile air race from St. Petersburg to Moscow during "Flying Week." Only one of the contenders actually reached Moscow. The following year, 1911, Reilly himself flew, as either a pilot or passenger, in the second St. Petersburg Flying Week. His aviation connections and interest helped bolster his credentials in Russian high society.

There was also at this time an intersection between aviation and Reilly's activities as a spy, at least in his later telling of the events. One story he disseminated related to an innovative German magneto, an engine-driven electrical generator that fired piston-engine aircraft spark plugs. At an air show in Frankfurt in 1910, a German plane went down and, according to Reilly, a British intelligence agent named Jones recruited him to assist, at some risk, in extracting the magneto from the wreckage, make drawings of it, and then replace it in the wrecked plane before anyone noticed. It sounds like a tall tale, but who knows?

What is certain is that Reilly's aviation activities helped him gain access to Russia's military-industrial complex. The Russo-Japanese war had ended with the destruction of the tsar's fleet, and much of what remained was obsolescent. The government decided to build a new, modern navy. Reilly befriended the adjutant to Minister of Marine I. K. Grigorovich, Lieutenant Petr Ivanovich Zalesskii, who incidentally had served in Port Arthur during the siege, and his beautiful young wife, Nadezhda (Nadia or Nadine) Petrovna (née Massino). She later told an agent of the United States government's Bureau of Investigation (later renamed the Federal Bureau of Investigation or FBI) that when she first set eyes on Reilly, she "immediately decided to have him." Reilly may have been equally enamored. By all accounts, Nadine was vivacious and charming. Reilly came to call her Kissenka or Kiska (kitten) and, in writing, referred to her as "K."

In 1918, after she moved to the United States and Reilly married her (as his second or third wife), a Bureau of Investigation agent described Nadine as "almost 29 years old, five foot three inches tall," of "slight build," weighing 112 pounds, with dark hair and "very much tanned." She had a "very attractive personality" and spoke "perfect French," though her English had a "pronounced accent."

Alongside his various pastimes and social networking, Reilly, soon after reaching St. Petersburg, began working freelance for Mendrokhovich & Lubenskii (M&L), a company that brokered military contracts for the Russian government. Reilly had ingratiated himself with Iosif Mendrokhovich, a Jew, and persuaded him that he, Reilly, could bag naval contracts with the German company Blohm & Voss (B&V) of Hamburg. These required Russian Ministry of Marine approval. Okhrana files at the time referred to Reilly as "the Broker." M&L quickly became the sole agents for B&V in Russia. Blohm & Voss were major shipbuilders—though ultimately, for the tsar, they built dry docks rather than ships, and Russia found shipbuilders elsewhere, primarily in the United Kingdom. B&V records show that Reilly occasionally dealt with the company directly, not through M&L. Quite naturally, Mendrokhovich was unhappy with this, and even complained to Blohm & Voss about "this stubborn man," who was constantly demanding higher commission fees. But M&L did not let him go. It was Reilly who "oiled the wheels"—that is, bribed Russian officials—and provided B&V with insider (Russian) information in order to firm up orders for their products. Reilly's activities included blackening Blohm & Voss rivals, keeping Blohm & Voss *au courant* with competition bids and orders, and getting Russian journalists to publish articles favoring B&V. Reilly made large commissions.

Reilly's positioning probably also made him invaluable to British intelligence. Through the Russian Ministry of Marine and B&V he likely had access to German naval construction thinking and plans, which no doubt made their way to London. En passant, Reilly also bagged Nadine. Margaret, who had initially joined Reilly, against his wishes, in St. Petersburg, refused to grant him a divorce, even after he offered her £10,000. Perhaps she had learned that he had married Anne Luke. But Margaret fairly quickly left St. Petersburg, perhaps fearing that she would end up like her first husband, the Reverend Thomas.

Margaret moved to France and then Belgium, while periodically nagging Reilly for money. Two decades after leaving St. Petersburg Margaret wrote that she had loved Reilly "with complete abandon, but that his many betrayals and affairs with other women had turned her love into hatred." At one point, she tried to commit suicide by shooting herself in the temple, but she botched it and the bullet sent her into a coma. When she woke after six weeks, doctors installed a glass eye in her right socket. This did not prevent her from volunteering to work on a Red Cross team that went to Bulgaria during the First Balkan War, in 1912. She spent the rest of her life in Europe, ending up as a governess in the Brussels household of an English expatriate, Robert Messenger, in the 1930s. Leon Messenger, Robert's son, remembered her as well read, "the perfect embodiment of a cultured lady." On walks in the woods she spoke with him of "the greatness of the British Empire and [of] the white man's burden," according to his 1985 article "The Nanny with the Glass Eye." Margaret died in Brussels during World War Two.

Back in pre–World War One St. Petersburg, Nadine's husband, Petr, was amenable to hard cash and, for a sum, agreed to let her go. But the divorce took years to mature. Nadine and Reilly eventually left Russia, traveling separately. Reilly landed in San Francisco in January 1915, and, a few weeks later Nadine landed in New York, where they eventually got back together.

During those prewar years in Russia, Reilly found time for missions on behalf of British intelligence elsewhere in Europe. In 1909, for example, working for Melville, he tried to cull intelligence on German armaments—at least, that is what he told some of his friends. Posing as Karl Hahn, a Baltic German, he took a job as a welder in the Krupps armaments factory in Essen. Within weeks, he broke into the factory's offices and photographed armaments production plans, which he passed on to London. In his telling, Reilly had to kill a guard during the operation.

But Reilly's spying escapades at this time clearly played second fiddle to his business ventures. Among other enterprises, he tried to relaunch a patent medicine company, which, interestingly, he named Rosenblum & Long, Manufacturers of Patent Medicines—resurrecting his original family name. Perhaps he felt that a Jewish moniker might help sell medicinal products. But the company failed to make a profit, and his partner Mr. Long apparently absconded with the firm's last £600. Perhaps Reilly wasn't quite as astute or devious as many believed—but he was saved from bankruptcy by a Jewish lawyer, a Mr. Abrahams.

Reilly's years of financially treading water—he failed to make the breakthrough to millionairedom—ended when the world, and in a sense he himself, went to war in 1914.

3

World War One

DURING 1914–1917, while the world was at war (primarily pitting Britain, Russia, France, and their affiliates against Germany, Austro-Hungary, and the Ottoman Empire), Reilly spent his days making money—from that war. To wage war, Russia—for much of the time with four-five million men under arms—required vast quantities of guns, munitions, motor vehicles, and other equipment. But its industrial base, while fast developing in the nineteenth century, was still very narrow. From 1914 on, the country imported much of what it needed, and Reilly saw himself as the man best suited for brokering the necessary deals. The purchases were enormous—and so were the broker's profits. In the course of the war Russia purchased more than 2.5 million rifles, hundreds of millions of bullets, more than 11 million artillery shells, 60,000 motor vehicles, 500 aircraft, and 800 locomotives. Once its industries had gone onto a war footing, the United States gradually became the Allies' chief arms supplier. By war's end, a full one-third of the munitions and equipment used by Russia was coming from the United States. Reilly was to play a not insignificant role in this trade.

In late June 1914, Reilly and Nadine were holidaying at St-Raphaël on the Riviera when the news broke: Gavrilo Princip, a Serbian student, had murdered Archduke Franz Ferdinand, the heir to the Austro-Hungarian imperial throne, unleashing weeks of diplomatic-military brinkmanship and, ultimately, the world war. Reilly immediately understood the business implications and rushed off to St. Petersburg, leaving Nadine literally stranded on the beach. The plan was that they would eventually meet up in New York.

Once in Russia, Reilly touched base with his prewar contacts, laying the groundwork for impending deals. He was fast and efficient. On August 8, 1914, days after Germany's declaration of war on Russia, Major-General Erdeli, of the Quartermaster's Division in the Russian General Staff, issued a "certificate" stating that "the British subject Sidney George Reilly" be given "assistance" in passage out of Russia as he had been "commissioned by the Chief Artillery Department to acquire material and articles of armaments for the needs of our Army." As his future (third or fourth) wife, Pepita Bobadilla, later put it, Reilly was "sent to America by the Russian Government to place contracts for arms and equipment."

Before leaving St. Petersburg, Reilly signed up with Abram Zhivotovskii, a financier and director of the Russo-Asiatic Bank. Zhivotovskii would provide the necessary letters of credit, bridging loans, or promissory notes to pay for arms bought and shipped from outside Russia—and Reilly would act as his agent. Reilly would garner commissions, 1 percent, 2 percent, maybe even 5 percent per contract. Indeed, once in the United States Reilly was able to organize multiple commissions—from the Russian purchaser, from the foreign manufacturer, and sometimes from shipping companies and other facilitators.

Zhivotovskii did not give Reilly a completely free hand. He affixed a "gift" to their partnership: his nephew I. T. Zhivotovskii, now installed as Reilly's secretary and aide—the old man wished to keep tabs on what his agent was up to. Reilly entrained for Vladivostok, the nephew in tow—though he was soon rid of him (we don't know at what stop on the journey). By design or otherwise, on the train was Captain Dmitri Vasiliev, the Russian naval attaché to Washington. Reilly would not have missed that opportunity for a tête-à-tête. At Vladivostok Reilly boarded a steamer bound for Japan. And there he cut his first deals, contracting with the Obashi Powder Company and the Nippon Celluloid and Artificial Silk Company to provide Russia with an indeterminate quantity of munitions and high explosives.

Reilly spent only a few weeks in Japan. His real goal was America, the industrial powerhouse, where he hoped to strike it rich. And perhaps military exports from the United States would not be limited to Russia. For Reilly, of course, was no Russian patriot. He had grown up amid its anti-Semites, had endured imprisonment by the Okhrana, and had since acquired a more fetching citizenship and loyalty, to Great Britain. But Reilly remained principally wedded to Reilly, and money. Some of his biographers have suggested that while in the Far East at this time Reilly made contact with German agents, such as Admiral Paul von Hintze, Berlin's man in Shanghai, with the idea of purchasing equipment for Germany in the United States and even supplying Germany with intelligence. But this seems unlikely, and there is no evidence to bear it up.

What is clear is that on December 26, 1914, Reilly boarded the SS *Persia* at Yokohama bound for San Francisco. A few weeks later he was in New York and had installed himself at 115 Broadway, where Abram Zhivotovskii had his American branch office. Later, he moved across the street, to the Equitable Building, at 120 Broadway, suite 2722, where he was to work until the end of his American sojourn. He also rented an apartment at 260 West 76th Street, though often he spent nights at the Gotham Hotel. (Later, after reportedly making millions of dollars, Reilly spent his nights at the luxurious Saint Regis Hotel on 5th Avenue.) Reilly hired a young American, Dale Upton Thomas, as his office manager. The Equitable housed the offices of a number of financiers and import-export companies, including the Charles R. Flint Arms Company, with whom Reilly would soon deal. Reilly teamed up with Samuel McRoberts, vice president of National City Bank—who was also eager to sell arms to Russia—and McRoberts appointed Reilly managing officer of the Allied Machinery Company, also based at 120 Broadway. Reilly thus simultaneously sat on the boards of various companies during his years stateside.

The multilingual Reilly soon connected with German diplomats and businessmen (Germany only went to war with the United States in April 1917) and Russian officials, including officers in the Russian missions to the US, principally the military purchasing mission in New York and the embassy in Washington. He also connected with British officials—diplomats and intelligence officers—who were keeping an eye on German (and Russian) activities in the United States, including arms and munitions purchases.

While some Flint Company executives were later to describe Reilly as "every inch a crook," they acknowledged that he had "tremendous influence" with the Russian government and tsarist court. One of Reilly's key contacts was General Eduard Karlovich Hermonius, who orchestrated Russian war purchases in England and, in a general way, also oversaw Russian military contracts in the United States. Hermonius was Nadine's uncle. The threesome often dined together at the Coq d'Or when the general was in New York.

Within weeks of settling in New York, Reilly clinched two important deals with the Remington Arms Union Metallic Cartridge Company—one for one million dollars' worth of small arms ammunition, the other for 1.2 million rifles. The contracts stated that Reilly was to receive $2.5 per rifle and $2.5 per thousand rounds of ammunition, in all amounting to some $300,000. He also brokered smaller deals, whether on behalf of Zhivotovskii or for himself. In 1915 it was reported that he had made a cool $20,000 (equivalent to some $200,000 in today's money) on the sale to Russia of the steamship *Nevada*.

But the big money was in the arms deals. In 1918 the Bureau of Investigation, headed by Bruce Bielaski, investigated Reilly's affairs as part of what the bureau defined as the "Reilly, Weinstein, and Jachalski Case." The investigation was launched at the request of the State Department. In September of that year a team of BI agents raided Reilly's offices at 120 Broadway (apparently without a warrant, while he was away in Russia trying to subvert the Bolshevik regime; see below). The BI also looked at Reilly's (and Alexandre Weinstein's) New York accounts at the Guarantee Trust Company and the National City Bank. Weinstein, fat and gap-toothed, was a Russian Jewish lawyer and businessman whom Reilly may have first encountered and befriended in Baku in the early 1900s.

In Reilly's office they found a hidden "large portmanteau." But it contained only batches of love letters sent by Nadine ("Kiska") from France, addressed to Reilly first in Tokyo, then in New York. Reilly's safe, however, was something else. The investigators, who arrived with "two Russian interpreters from the Quartermaster's Department," found a stack of letters and contracts depicting Reilly's business dealings during the previous three years. "From the importance of the contracts and the vast amounts involved, it is apparent that Reilly must have had tremendous political backing in Russia," wrote Chief Yeoman Bond to his superiors in the bureau in his report of September 10, 1918. Among other items there was a contract between Reilly and the Nippon Celluloid and Artificial Silk Company from

December 26, 1914, for "smokeless powder"; a letter of June 15, 1916, to Reilly from a Mr. McCollum promising a commission for the deal signed with the British American Chemical Company of Montreal; a contract between Reilly and the Allis-Chalmers Transportation Company from November 24, 1916, providing for a commission on "every car purchased by the Russian Government"; and a contract from June 7, 1916, between Reilly and the Eddystone Ammunition Corporation awarding Reilly twenty-five cents for each three-inch shell going to Russia.

The deals were not always smooth sailing, however. There were almost always production and logistical snags. Sometimes manufacturers were unable to meet contractual deadlines; here and there, shipping problems arose. A major potential problem was posed at the Russian end—by munitions deemed flawed or unsuitable for Russian guns. Reilly had to overcome persistent hurdles posed by the military quality-control inspectorate at the Russian ports, often with the help of bribes.

A hint of some of the problems encountered was provided in Reilly's second contract with the Remington company. In it, Reilly was specifically charged with assisting "in the performance of said contract and in particular in reaching an understanding with the Russian Government as to the assurances required" and to "smooth over any disputes or questions that may arise."

Throughout 1915–1918, Reilly also had to contend with American competitors, who themselves sought to bag the lucrative Russian contracts. Reilly's primary rival was the J. Pierpont Morgan Bank and its affiliates and agents, who sought to corner—and largely succeeded in cornering—the vast market for American arms and munitions sales to all the Allies, not just to Russia. Still, Reilly also managed to make money, lots of it, in large measure due to his connections and, perhaps, acumen.

It was often to "Uncle" Hermonius that Reilly turned when deals he was trying to secure were frustrated by American competitors or Russian bureaucrats. On December 21, 1915, for example, he complained to the general that the Russian military authorities in Petrograd (called St. Petersburg before September 1914 and Leningrad from 1924) were ill-informed about American production capabilities and that obstructive overinspection was hindering the delivery process. Much money, he wrote, was wasted on "correspondence and telegrams," and he noted that "inspectors have been ordered to look round [American] factories, legal consultants have been . . . drawing up contracts, [and] in many cases draft, preliminary or even final agreements have been signed (and then torn up)—but . . . orders for rifles and cartridges have still not been placed." (Reilly tactfully refrained from mentioning the funds expended on bribes.) And when orders were placed, either they could not be fulfilled by American manufacturers or were duplicated, or provided munitions and guns unsuitable for Russia's needs. Reilly wrote that by December 1915 the Allies had placed orders in the United States for 7.5 million rifles, 3,500 million cartridges, and 1.5 million gun barrels, which American manufacturers had contracted for but, overreaching, had proved unable to meet.

Another problem for Reilly and the American manufacturers was active interference by German agents—through sabotage. On the night of July 29–30, 1916, huge explosions rocked the poorly guarded facilities on Black Tom Island, some two miles south of Manhattan, where more than 13,000 tons of explosives—mostly destined for Russia—were stored. There were two blasts, one in a railroad car, the other in a barge moored nearby. Shells flew through the air, windows shattered throughout lower Manhattan, burglar alarms went off, water mains burst, telephone lines went dead, and Brooklyn Bridge swayed. Later, in March 1917, Kurt Jahnke, the German agent who ran the sabotage ring, apparently blew up part of the US naval shipyard in Mare Island, California. And on April 11 he may have organized the destruction, by bomb and fire, of the Eddystone

Ammunition Corporation plant in Eddystone, Pennsylvania, a subsidiary of the Baldwin Locomotive Company, where Samuel Vauclain, a Reilly competitor for Russian purchases, was vice president. The Eddystone fire destroyed the plant—and killed 139 employees, mostly women and girls. It may have been an accident; but American and British officials suspected that Jahnke was responsible. The fire apparently began at the work station of one Fiodor Wozniak, a Ukrainian who may have been working for the Germans. Jahnke and his assistant Lothar Witzke were possibly responsible for the January 1917 explosion in Kingsland, New Jersey, at the Canadian Car and Foundry Company plant, which destroyed 500,000 three-inch shells destined for the Allies.

Jahnke was directly controlled by the German consul-general in San Francisco, Franz Bopp. The various explosions apparently cost Reilly a number of serious commissions. Jahnke and Witzke fled to Mexico in April 1917, when the United States entered the war on the Allied side. (For Jahnke it was thereafter all downhill. He returned to Germany, tried and failed in a number of business ventures, worked for a time for the Nazis, and was executed by the Soviets in 1945 after they conquered Germany.)

In either late February or April 1915, Reilly and Nadine traveled from New York to Petrograd possibly via Port Arthur and the Trans-Siberian Railway. According to some reports, in Japan or Shanghai Reilly collected Anne Luke and her two daughters and then deposited them in the Russian capital, in the care of friends in the local British community. She was calling herself at this time Anna Yanovna Reile. While in Petrograd Reilly apparently persuaded the Russian Red Cross to order a shipment of American ambulances. Back in the States, Reilly signed a deal with Mackenzie Manufacturing Company of Toronto for five million shells, earning him a $2.5 million commission.

In 1916, Reilly was joined in New York by some of his former business associates from Russia and the Far East. According to Colonel R. H. Van Deman, the chief of the American Military Intelligence Branch in the War Department, Alexandre Weinstein, with whom Reilly had bonded in St. Petersburg in 1909, entered the United States on July 16, 1916. "[Weinstein now] . . . represented a syndicate of Russian banks for the purpose of purchasing metals and chemicals," according to Van Deman. Weinstein opened an account with Chandler Brothers and deposited $47,500. In 1917, according to American intelligence, Weinstein "entered into a partnership with Sidney Reilly . . . [the] purchasing agent for the Allies." Bureau of Investigation officers wrote that Weinstein had a "bad" reputation, often referring to him as a former "brothel keeper." But this appears not to have posed a problem in the banking world. In 1916, the Russian-Asiatic Bank wrote to New York's National City Bank introducing their "esteemed customer" Weinstein and informed the American bank that "he has purchased in London . . . many hundred thousand pounds of material through the Russo-Asiatic Bank."

Many of Reilly's dealings were complicated and labyrinthine. In mid-1916 they came under growing scrutiny when allegations of overpayment, mismanagement, and corruption were hurled at members of the Russian purchasing mission in New York, officially called the Russian Supply Committee (RSC). Much of Reilly's business was conducted with or in coordination with the committee. Quite naturally, some of the allegations rubbed off on Reilly himself. In 1919, W. H. Courtenay, a retired British army colonel, wrote to British General Staff (Intelligence) that "Riley, a Jew whose real name is not believed to be 'Riley,'" in 1915 did "a lot of 'grafting' business [in New York] . . . and was party to sending bad ammunition to Russia. He was in fact believed to be in German pay, and the old [i.e., tsarist] Russian authorities denounced him more than once." (How a retired colonel came about such "information" is unclear.) Colonel Winfield Proskey, an engineer at Flint & Company, told the Bureau of Investigation at one point that the British naval attaché in Washington, Captain Guy Gaunt, said that Reilly was involved in trying to sell "300,000 discarded [malfunctioning?] Krug-Jergensen [Krag-Jørgensen] rifles" to the Russians.

Some of this may have been true. But there was probably little truth to the additional charge that Reilly was "in German pay," and it is unclear who in Russia had denounced him as a German agent. But to be sure, there were Russian officials, fed information by Morgan banking executives, American officials, or British intelligence officers, who didn't take to him.

In August 1916, the RSC's head, General A. V. Sapozhnikov, a Reilly ally, was replaced by General A. P. Zaliubovskii, who was mandated to clean up the purchasing operations in America. On Zaliubovskii's staff was a Lieutenant Boris Brasol, a zealous investigator and plainspeaking anti-Semite, whom Reilly took pains to neutralize. Brasol had been a junior prosecutor in the infamous Beilis blood libel case back in Russia in 1911–1913. Menachem Beilis, a Russian Jew, was accused and tried—and in the end acquitted—of the ritual murder of a thirteen-year-old Christian Ukrainian boy. Reilly plied (actually, bribed) Brasol with intelligence about alleged American-Jewish financing of German arms purchases. He may also have given Brasol money. As to Zaliubovskii, Reilly worked diligently to subvert him after his appointment as head of the purchasing mission. Alfred Knox, Britain's military attaché in Petrograd—and a future Reilly ally—complained that Zaliubovskii was "ignorant and difficult"; like Reilly, he called for Sapozhnikov's reinstatement. But this didn't happen.

The French military mission in the United States also suspected that Reilly was a German agent. Nonetheless, the SIS station in New York joined Reilly in helping to blunt the investigation by Zaliubovskii's staff. The accusations focused on Colonel A. V. Nekrasov, perhaps Reilly's chief contact in the Russian mission. The investigators, who included non-Russians such as deputy SIS chief in New York Norman Graham Thwaites, eventually approached Reilly. Over lunch with Thwaites, Reilly gave Nekrasov a clean bill of health. The lunch was also attended by Weinstein, as Thwaites later related in his autobiography. However, the BI put a quite different spin on that lunch. In its report from 1918, the bureau wrote that Thwaites "had lunched with both Reilly and Weinstein and they had aroused his suspicions in their efforts to get Nekrassov out of trouble." In his memoirs, Thwaites wrote, somewhat contrarily, that "our Russian friends [i.e., Nekrasov et al.] were giving themselves a good time in the hospitable city on the Hudson, but I could find no evidence either of graft or of enemy [i.e., German] contacts."

Reilly's life in New York, as elsewhere during his later years, was multifaceted. Aside from his business dealings, Reilly dabbled in intelligence, which he collected from his many and varied contacts. In 1916–1917 he appears to have furnished the SIS team in New York, headed by Lt. Col. William Wiseman, with tidbits of information about arms deals and about Russian and German personnel working the American scene. This proved to be the start of Reilly's direct connection to SIS, which two years later turned into official employment. Years later, Thwaites was to write of Reilly's "excellent intelligence work" and "valuable services" to British intelligence in New York.

But other British officials in the United States were not as enraptured. Captain (later Admiral) Gaunt, suspecting that Reilly was secretly helping the Germans, called him "an enemy of the Allies." (Incidentally, Gaunt at the time also denounced, in similar terms, Leon Trotsky, who had arrived in the US in January 1917. On his way back to Russia in April, Trotsky was briefly detained by the Canadian authorities in Halifax, Nova Scotia—but then almost immediately released due to the unlikely intervention of the SIS. Whether Reilly had a hand in this we don't know, though given his knowledge of Russian affairs he may have been consulted on whether to hold or release the revolutionary.) The paths of these two Jews were to cross the following year.

Reilly spent much of his time in New York subverting possible American-Russian arms deals sired by other middlemen, primarily Morgan Bank associates. American officers later complained to British intelligence officials that it was "impossible to do anything [with the Russians] unless it was done through Reilly." They called Reilly "a clever schemer."

At the end of the day, Reilly's dealings with Germany and Germans, if there were any, during his stay in the United States are unclear. A variety of officials and agencies believed that he was (a) spying for the Germans, (b) purchasing arms and munitions for Germany, and (c) obstructing arms and munitions shipments to the Allies, perhaps even to the extent of abetting sabotage operations on American soil. Flint engineer Proskey, for example, called Reilly "one of the most astute and dangerous international spies now at large." Another Flint man, John F. Cordley, said Reilly would "do anything for the almighty dollar."

There appears to be a very small element of truth in all of this. In the course of 1915, Reilly brokered a number of deals in which some of the matériel exported from the United States had ended up in German hands. But it is unclear if Reilly had had prior knowledge of this. In 1916, Reilly arranged the purchase by the Russian War Ministry of 700 tons of nickel ore from the Vanadium Company of Pittsburgh. The original source of the ore was a company owned by Basil Zaharoff. The ore was eventually shipped via Stockholm. Only 200 tons reached Russia; the rest, or some of the rest, was siphoned off to Germany. Similarly, a Reilly-brokered deal with the Allied Machinery Company (AMC)—a subsidiary of the American International Corporation—saw shipments of machine tools destined for Russia ending up in Germany rather than Petrograd. Reilly sat on the board of directors of AMC.

Even more than Reilly himself, several Reilly associates were fingered as German agents. Thwaites at one point reported to London that Weinstein was "in touch with prominent Germans." Antoine Jachalski (aka Tony Farraway), another European businessman–cum–con man, was long suspected by American investigators of being a German agent. Jachalski, who spent the war years in the United States, told several of his mistresses (like Reilly, he was a flagrant womanizer and gambler) that he had a brother who was an Austrian officer. By 1917, with spy fever taking a firm hold on the American imagination, this was serious grounds for suspicion. One of Jachalski's mistresses, Peggy Marsh, a chorus girl, told BI agents that Jachalski appeared to be a German spy and had tried to get her to extract intelligence for him from American businessmen and army officers.

Consequent on these allegations and suspicions, the BI, an arm of the Department of Justice, supported by the Military Intelligence Division and the Office of Naval Intelligence (which itself was assisted by private citizens belonging to the American Protective League, a volunteer group of patriots), launched a serious investigation of Reilly and his associates in spring 1917. The investigation proved long, amateurish, and complex, given Reilly's (and Weinstein's and Jachalski's) widespread connections and complicated business ventures spanning a number of continents, and the fact that from mid-1917 Reilly himself was absent in Canada for much of the time. The bureau's investigation was overlaid with a clear patina of anti-Semitism. In its interim summary of the investigation ("Memorandum No. 2") from August 1918, bureau executives wrote: "They are all blackguards," referring to the coterie of Russian arms-procuring businessmen surrounding and including Reilly. "[They were] all Russian Jewish men who in some extraordinary way obtained direct contracts from the Russian Government and made fat profits." In a subsequent summary, the bureau concluded: "These men are international confidence men of the highest class."

In their September 1918 raid on Reilly's Broadway offices, the BI investigators found check stubs of payments made to Weinstein (for $6,000) and Jachalski (for $2,000). But they found nothing to substantiate accusations of fraud or malfeasance. Certainly they found nothing that showed that Reilly (or Weinstein or Jachalski) had worked for Germany or abetted its war effort. The bureau may have concluded, in January 1919, that the threesome were high-class con men, but the investigation was ultimately a waste of man-hours and turned up what amounted to a hill of beans. The bureau found nothing to show a Reilly-Germany connection or that Reilly had defrauded the Russian government or deliberately sold it damaged goods. (Nevertheless, the investigation provided later researchers, like myself, with a great deal of information, some of it even true, about Reilly's life and dealings in America.)

The suspicions and investigations notwithstanding, by 1917 Reilly had earned upward of $2 million (some $20 million in today's money) in commissions, according to an SIS report from March 1918. (One Reilly biographer, Andrew Cook, wrote that Reilly's earnings "by 1917 . . . were well over $3 million.") Moreover, a number of banks and manufacturers, according to Reilly, owed him additional sums. So by 1917, Reilly was a wealthy man. But while in New York and during the following years, he squandered it all. He traveled constantly and gambled heavily, and often lost, and generally lived the good life—with chauffeur-driven cars, shows and parties every night, and expensive hotels and restaurants frequented on a daily basis. In the evenings, he often ate, gambled, and partied with Jachalski, Weinstein, and Moisei Ginsburg, who had joined Weinstein in New York soon after his arrival. He also accumulated objets d'art. And during the early 1920s, Reilly also expended large sums on his and others' anti-Bolshevik activities (see below).

Of course, Reilly spent a great deal of time—and money—

on his women as well. He may have successfully left Margaret stranded in Europe—where she reportedly worked in 1915–1916 with the Red Cross in Paris and then Belgium. But in February 1915, barely giving Reilly a day's notice, Nadine arrived in New York from France aboard the SS *Rochambeau*. She was intent on at last clinching the marriage: what Reilly had promised her, she was bent on setting in stone. She came ashore without a visa—but only after cabling a warning to the New York City Police Department that Reilly was violating the Mann Act, the anti–white slavery law from 1910 forbidding the transportation, or importation, of women—such as herself—for "immoral purposes." Reilly was waiting at the pier—and next to him were a handful of New York detectives. It must have been discombobulating in the extreme. Nadine came down the gangplank and a three-cornered "discussion" ensued. By its end, the detectives, in effect, ordered Reilly to marry Nadine or be dragged off to jail. The upshot was a type of shotgun wedding. On February 16, the happy couple were married in the Manhattan registry office. A proper religious ceremony followed at St. Nicholas Russian Orthodox Cathedral, presided over by the church's New York bishop. Nadine was apparently born Jewish, but her parents subsequently converted to Christianity and she had followed suit. At the registry office, both witnesses were Russian officials; at the church, Reilly and Nadine hosted friends, but there were no relatives from either side. At some point afterward, Reilly gave his bride "a wonderful collection of jade," according to George Hill, who was to spy for Britain in Russia alongside Reilly in 1918–1919.

Once (re)married, however, Reilly was off and running. According to Bureau of Investigation agents, during the following years in New York Reilly had a string of affairs with young women, including Olive Thomas, a Ziegfeld Follies girl; Clara Kimball Young, a silent movies starlet; and Beatrice

Madeleine Tremaine, a twenty-two-year-old would-be actress. The last seems to have been the most serious relationship. Reilly met Tremaine in 1916 at Lucille's, a dressmaker, where she modeled. She and several of her friends and co-workers were repeatedly questioned by BI agents during 1918. One of her co-workers described Tremaine as a "most skilled and dangerous liar." The bureau had her followed for days on end. She even complained about it to Reilly, who at one point hired "two Pinkerton detectives" to shadow her, to deter the BI shadowers. Reilly gave her a $200 monthly allowance and paid for her acting lessons; for months, "he maintained her" in a bungalow in Santa Barbara, California; he sent her to a "finishing" school, Miss Beard's School in Orange, New Jersey; and at one point, she claimed, Reilly even proposed, saying that he was about to divorce Nadine. The American investigators referred to Tremaine as Reilly's "ward." The BI also constantly tailed Nadine and even had one of its agents, a "Miss Baltis," befriend her, swimming and lunching with her on Long Island. The BI reported that Nadine was still "in love with Reilly" and was very jealous of Tremaine.

But Reilly's successes with women may not have been all clear sailing. According to one Reilly—and Tremaine—friend interviewed by the BI, Dolores Rose, an English-born chorus girl, Reilly was "a man very much disliked by women but unusually attractive to men." This may have been a lie to put the BI agents off the scent, for whatever reason—or it may have been a heartfelt, albeit minority, opinion.

Be that as it may, Tremaine apparently developed a fondness for, and intimate relationship with, the engineer Tony Jachalski, the Polish-Jewish Moscow-born fixer who had spent months traveling around the United States and whom many who knew him—including BI agents—suspected of being a German spy. His various girlfriends, interviewed by the BI, reported that he had photographed "bridges, roads, military depots, etc." in the western United States and associated with American army officers. In the end, authorities in Texas imprisoned Jachalski for "over six" months and subjected him to lengthy interrogations. In New York, Jachalski had reportedly been intimate with actresses Gertrude Grimes and Nita Naldi (originally Nonna Dooley, who later was awarded a star in Hollywood's Walk of Fame). And he also spent nights with Nadine, as her maid Alice Todd revealed to bureau investigators. (Weinstein also reportedly spent a great deal of time with Nadine, though here the relations were ultimately deemed by the BI "platonic.")

But Jachalski emerged from the protracted BI investigation clean as a whistle and was released from military detention in November 1918. The following year, an embarrassed BI was forced to admit to the State Department that, after investigating Jachalski in "a most thorough manner," it had "failed to develop any definite [incriminating] evidence" that he had spied or was spying for the Germans or that he had in any way helped the Germans during the war. But they continued to maintain that he was "a suspicious character," given his apparently unaccountable wealth and dissipated ways.

As for Nadine, Reilly divorced her in Paris in 1920. She went on to marry Gustav Högman, of the Swedish Nobel (prizes) family, though apparently she had money of her own as her father owned oil in Baku. (The Nobels, too, had made oil money in Baku.) She appears to have died in Switzerland around 1950.

All in all, Reilly's years in New York had been very fruitful. He had amassed a small fortune and a string of new lovers. But Reilly always wanted something more—that is, to leave his mark on history. And making money and collecting mistresses, while the nations of the earth were engaged in a life-and-death struggle, didn't quite cut it. The years in New York had been staid and enjoyable, but they were ultimately characterized by inertia. He was getting nowhere. He had enjoyed the scheming and hustling of the arms deals and the equipping of far-off armies for battle. But he aspired to more immediate relevance and higher things—and within months, as it turned out, Reilly was to position himself on the very cusp of changing the course of history.

4

The Reilly/Lockhart Plot

HAVING SPENT most of World War One making money in the United States, Reilly decided to return to Europe—for him, still the center of the world—and resume some of his prewar preoccupations. More specifically, he now sought to convert his amateur or at least part-time dabbling in espionage into a proper, full-time career. He clearly enjoyed spying, and thrived on the dangers involved and on overcoming them. Like all spies, he enjoyed the sense of belonging to an elite and exclusive community, of those who knew what the vast multitudes were ignorant of. Reilly set his sights on British intelligence—and its officers in New York, it appears, encouraged him. Over the following months they were to facilitate the realization of his aspirations.

On March 13, 1917, Reilly enlisted in the Canadian branch of Britain's Royal Flying Corps, soon to be renamed the Royal Air Force (RAF). The enlistment, in Toronto, was probably arranged by Norman Thwaites, the number-two man in MI6's

New York station. It is unclear what training, if any, Reilly actually received in Canada, as an airman or in another capacity, or whether, indeed, he spent any substantial time in that country.

In August, Reilly entered Russia, via Arkhangelsk, and was attached to the British military mission based there, assisting Russia's faltering war effort with supplies and advice. Reilly then made his way to the capital, Petrograd—which another British spy, the writer William Somerset Maugham, described as "dingy, sordid, and dilapidated"—and established (or reestablished) contact with a variety of officials and officers. Russia had radically changed. The war years had plunged the country into a protracted military, political, and economic crisis, and in March 1917 a popular revolution (the so-called February Revolution, dated according to the old calendar) had ousted the tsar and installed a moderate socialist-liberal regime in place of the monarchy. In July, the leader of the moderate wing of the Socialist Revolutionary Party, Alexander Kerensky, took over as chairman of the cabinet (prime minister). The new government, apart from social and economic reforms, wanted Russia to soldier on, as one of the Allies, in the war against Germany. It was opposed by the radical Bolsheviks, led by Vladimir Ilyich Ulyanov, or Lenin, who advocated immediate Russian withdrawal from the war and from the alliance. R. H. Bruce Lockhart, the diplomat about to be appointed as London's representative to the Bolsheviks, later described Lenin—"short of stature, rather plump . . . broad shoulders, round, red face, high intellectual forehead . . . he looked at first glance more like a provincial grocer than a leader of men"—as a man with "steely eyes . . . half-contemptuous, half-smiling . . . unscrupulous and as uncompromising as a Jesuit." On November 7, the Bolsheviks overthrew Kerensky's provisional government in a well-organized, effectively bloodless coup d'état known as the October Revolution (again according to the old calendar). The coup had been organized by Trotsky.

Three weeks earlier, on October 19, probably to enhance his status while operating in Russia, MI6 arranged for Reilly—who as far as we know was not yet on the agency's staff—to be given a temporary commission as a second lieutenant in the Royal Flying Corps. That month he attended an "aviation conference" being held in Petrograd—either dressed as an RFC second lieutenant or in mufti, in the guise of a merchant calling himself Konstantin Massino—and hobnobbed with Russian officers and officials. It is not clear if Reilly was there representing the RFC or MI6 or British military intelligence. Also attending the proceedings was Captain George Alexander Hill, known as "Pop," an SIS officer (code-named IK.8). The Russian-born Hill—his father had been a British businessman in Russia—initially went to Russia for British military intelligence, then stayed there undercover serving the SIS, for a time even assuming the position of "air advisor" to the newly appointed Bolshevik commissar for war, Trotsky. Earlier during the war, Hill had trained in the RFC as a pilot. It was said that he was "the first man to land spies by plane behind enemy lines (in the Balkans)." (Later, during World War Two, with the rank of brigadier-general, he served in Moscow as the Special Operations Executive's liaison with the NKVD. The SOE was a clandestine British sabotage and intelligence organization set up by Churchill at the start of that conflict to liaise with European resistance movements and direct behind-the-lines operations against the Nazis.)

That autumn, the two British spies, Reilly and Hill, set about recruiting agents, "cultivating and corrupting" (in Hill's phrase) officials of the new revolutionary regime, including Vladimir Grigorevich Orlov, a former military prosecutor; Ivan Manasevich-Manuilov, journalist; and Alexander Alexandrovich Yakushev, of the Ministry of Ways and Communications, later an aide of Trotsky's. Thus, though not yet officially an employee of SIS, Reilly laid the foundation for the network that was to serve him well, as an MI6 officer, during his historic exploits in Petrograd and Moscow the following year.

By the start of 1918, Reilly was back in London. He walked about in his RFC uniform and lodged at the Savoy Hotel—and formally applied for a position in MI6. He wrote to a "Col. Byron" at the War Office, enclosing letters of recommendation. One was from the director and "Chief Constructor" T. G. Owens Thurston, of Vickers, a large British arms manufacturer, attesting to Reilly's "great abilities as a linguist," extensive knowledge of Russia, and diplomatic skills. Immediately after receiving the application, on January 19, MI6 asked MI5 whether Reilly was "OK from your point of view." MI5's Major Anson responded that they had "nothing recorded against Sidney George Reilly" and that the police, too, had "nothing" against him.

But MI6, having heard rumors of Reilly's dubious reputation, sought further assurances. At MI6's behest, MI5 began a vetting procedure, even putting a tail on the subject. MI5 emerges from its reports looking like the Keystone Kops. On March 7, according to one of its agents, "Reilly . . . disappeared in the direction of Pall Mall." A.L.W. tried to follow, but a "[taxi] driver informed A.L.W. that as his was only a two cylinder and the one Reilly was in was a four cylinder," it was "useless to try and catch him." The following day proved no better: "Reilly got in [a taxi] and it sounded as if he gave [the] Savoy Hotel [as the destination]. No taxi being available, we followed on a bus"—but once there, the shadowers failed to find him. In all, the surveillance produced "nothing much, owing to the fact that Reilly usually moved about in taxis, and it was nearly always impossible to get another cab in which to follow." Moreover, the agent in question chided his superiors, he was "told nothing, neither the reason for the action I was asked to take, nor any information about [Reilly]. In these circumstances it is extremely difficult to act without the person concerned in some way becoming aware of what is happening. It would simplify matters and prevent unavoidable mistakes if in future cases of this sort more information was given [to the agents in the field]."

Nonetheless, MI5 produced a report. Reilly was described as an "Irishman" born in Clonmel in 1874. "He is said to be very respectable and pays his bills [i.e., £8.80 per week at lodgings in 22 Ryder Street, SW, to which he had moved from the Savoy on January 10] quite regularly." He had few visitors. "It is said that he rarely leaves his rooms before after [*sic*] mid-day, and usually returns about tea time, and goes out in the evening to dinner." He was always back in by midnight. It shouldn't have been very difficult to track Reilly: he spent much of his time dining or taking coffee at the Savoy and the Ritz, and he usually wore a carnation or rose in his buttonhole, purchased in "Solomon's flower shop in St. James' Street."

MI6 had also instituted inquiries in New York. MI6's New York station responded: "Reilly is a British subject . . . who has made money since the beginning of the war through . . . corrupted members of the Russian Purchasing Commission . . . We consider him untrustworthy and unsuitable to [the] work suggested." In a further cable from MI6 New York, Reilly was described as "a shrewd businessman of undoubted ability but without patriotism or principles and therefore not recommended for any position which requires loyalty as he would not hesitate to use it to further his own commercial interests." Reilly was also described as "unscrupulous" and with connections in Germany, Japan, and Russia. Fair enough—but MI6's New York station then formally supported his recruitment! It is unclear why the station did this despite the negative opinions it had earlier proffered.

London's intelligence bureaucracy spent the next few days scratching its head. New alarm bells were set off by a telegram, intercepted by the London censor's office, from Reilly to Maxim Litvinov, the Bolshevik representative in London, asking for a meeting. MI5 shot off two cables—one to the British army in Ireland, who responded that there was no trace of Sidney Reilly's birth in Clonmel (though there had once been "a Band-master named Wm. Reilly," of "the old South Tipperary Mili-tia," who had had five sons—but none of them appeared to be Sidney George Reilly); and the other to Metropolitan Police assistant commissioner Basil Thomson, in charge of Scotland Yard's Special Branch. Thomson replied by asking whether he should "institute inquiries." Alerted, MI6 told MI5: "No thank you. We know about the [Litvinoff] telegram, and it is all right." MI5 instructed Thomson to stand down.

In the end, none of this brouhaha affected Sir Mansfield Cumming ("C"), head of MI6. Given the complex situation in Russia, the country's current importance as a wavering war-making ally or rogue power, and its prospective role in the postwar world, the MI6 chief was desperate to obtain good in-telligence on that country. As C put it in his diary a few months later, "Russia will be the most important country for us in fu-ture and we should sow seed and strike roots [there] now."

Proper vetting was not exactly the norm in MI6 (or MI5) at this time—or, in fact, two decades later, when the treacherous Cambridge circle, Kim Philby and company, were inducted into the two organizations. During late 1917 and early 1918, C sent a cluster of officers, many of them not of the usual MI6 "old boy" genre (that is, from respectable, landed-gentry fami-lies, graduates of Eton or Harrow or Oxbridge, veterans of Guards regiments), into Russia, and he was none too picky about their provenance. Indeed, C often exhibited a penchant for the ec-centric (he was one himself) and the exotic. As intelligence his-torian Christopher Andrew observed about William Wiseman, head of MI6's New York station and another C recruit, he was "just the sort of adventurous, resourceful, capable, clubbable maverick who appealed to C." Apart from the "clubbable," Reilly also fit the bill. But in Reilly's case, there was a constrain-ing factor which C had to, and did, overcome: his probable Jewishness. C, like most of his class, often exhibited knee-jerk anti-Semitism, as seen in a heads-up cable he sent in late March 1918 informing the British mission in Petrograd of Reilly's imminent arrival: "On 25 March," he wrote, "Sydney George Reilli [*sic*] . . . leaves for Archangel from England. Jewish-Jap type, brown eyes very protruding, deeply lined sallow face, may be bearded . . . He has sixteen diamonds value 640.7.2 [pounds, shillings, pence] as most useful currency." Note the (perhaps subconscious) linkage between "the Jewish-Jap type" and money (diamonds). C's officers in New York exhibited similar attitudes, as in this cable: "Reilly is a British subject married to a Russian Jewess . . . We consider him untrustworthy." And two weeks later, on March 20, they added: "R. is [a] Greek Jew; very clever; entirely unscrupulous."

By then, though, C had already made up his mind and summoned Reilly. They met, for the first time, in the chief's office at 2 Whitehall Court on March 15.

It is worth looking for a moment at the man who was hiring Reilly. Mansfield George Smith had married Leslie Marion Valiant Cumming (known as May) in 1889. He then, very unconventionally, began to call himself Mansfield Smith Cumming; eventually, he shortened his name to Mansfield Cumming, and then shortened it still further to the legendary C, which is how he thenceforth signed his dispatches and reports, in bright green ink. (Duplicating this practice, in the James Bond movies MI6's chief is called and signs in as M.)

C was born in England in 1859 to a landed-gentry family, one of whose ancestors, Sir Michael Carrington, had been standard-bearer to King Richard I (the Lionheart) in the Third Crusade and, after playing an instrumental role in the conquest of Acre, died in the Holy Land. At age twelve, C was sent off to the Britannia Royal Naval College in Dartmouth, and he subsequently pursued an undistinguished career in the Senior Service, ending up as a flag leftenant in 1885. His service record described him as "unfit" for further service as he suffered from seasickness. He spent the following decade in business, but may on the side have occasionally provided services for the Admiralty's Naval Intelligence Department. In 1898, he rejoined the Royal Navy on "the active retired list," mainly working on boom defenses, specifically the defenses of Southampton port. He was in effect a washed-up naval officer. But then, a decade later, in 1909, the completely unexpected happened: out of the blue, at the suggestion of the navy (where he had one powerful patron, Rear Admiral A. E. Bethell, director of Naval Intelligence), he was asked by the War Office to set up the Secret Service Bureau (SSB). The SSB was to be charged with both counterintelligence and foreign intelligence gathering. It is unclear why Cumming, a semiretired naval part-timer, was chosen; indeed, it remains one of the enduring mysteries concerning the birth of the SIS (MI6).

The chief impetus for setting up the SSB was the growing sense that Germany was turning into a powerful potential enemy, perhaps even capable of challenging the Royal Navy's supremacy on the oceans and invading Britain itself, coupled with the realization that Britain's existing intelligence agencies—the Naval Intelligence Department and the War Office's MO2 and MO3, minute subsections within the Directorate of Military Operations—were insufficient for the tasks at hand. At War Office insistence, Cumming was *ab initio* paired with Vernon Kell, and the two became the SSB's co-founders. Kell was a career War Office intelligence officer with a cosmopolitan upbringing, fluent in German and French and able to get along in Russian and Chinese. He was placed in charge of the counterintelligence section of the SSB, which in 1910, when the bureau split into two organizations, became the Security Service or MI5, with Kell remaining as chief until 1940. Cumming, meanwhile, was placed in charge of SSB's foreign intelligence section, which, when the bureau split, became the Secret Intelligence Service or MI6 (initially referred to as MI1c). Cumming was to head MI6 until his death in 1923.

The SSB, set up from scratch, worked out of cramped, rented premises in the West End. Over the following years, Cumming and Kell slowly built up their respective services, personally hiring agent after agent, secretary after secretary.

C, who fairly quickly turned MI6 into a world-spanning organization with hundreds of staff and agents, became a legendary figure already in his lifetime. One of the highlights of his career involved a road accident in France during World War One, in which his son Alastair, who was driving, died and he, reputedly, ended up cutting off his own leg below the knee to escape the wreckage of their Rolls-Royce.

Sir Samuel Hoare, a Conservative cabinet minister in the 1920s and 1930s, was, for a time during World War One, SIS's station chief in Russia. He described Cumming as "jovial and very human, bluff and plain-speaking, outwardly, at least, a very simple man . . . physically and mentally the very antithesis of the spy king of popular fiction. Cumming mixed a lightness of character—a live-wire of boisterous, outgoing nature and a great tease with the children—with a morose severity once in office."

A daring wartime MI6 operative, Paul Dukes (code-named "ST25"), whose cover was assistant conductor at Petrograd's Imperial Mariinsky Theatre, later described C and his office at their first meeting in August 1918:

> The writing desk was so placed with the window behind it that on entering everything appeared only in silhouette. It was some seconds before I could distinguish things. A row of half a dozen extending telephones stood at the left of a big desk littered with papers. On a side table were numerous maps and drawings, with models of seaplanes, submarines and mechanized devices, while a row of bottles of various colours and a distilling outfit with a rack of test tubes bore witness to

chemical experiments and operations. These evidences of scientific investigations only served to intensify an already overpowering atmosphere of strangeness and mystery. But it was not these things that engaged my attention as I stood nervously waiting. . . . My eyes fixed themselves on the figure at the writing table . . . his shoulders hunched, with his head supported on one hand, busily writing. [He] sat in his shirt sleeves. . . . This extraordinary man was short of stature, thick set, with grey hair covering a well-rounded head. His mouth was stern, an eagle eye, full of vivacity, [he] glanced—or glared, as the case might be—piercingly through a gold-rimmed monocle. The coat that hung over the back of the chair was that of a naval officer.

Reilly left us no record of his first meeting with Cumming. But C did: "Major [John] Scale introduced Mr. Reilly, who is willing to go to Russia for us. Very clever—very doubtful—has been everywhere and done everything." C instructed that Reilly be given £1,250 in cash and diamonds to fund his sojourn and operations—"[though] I must agree . . . it is a great gamble," C jotted down in his diary. Nonetheless, a few days later, accompanied by the organization's Claude Dansey ("Colonel Z"), C motored to the City to purchase the diamonds. From then on, in MI6's books, Reilly was "ST1." Cumming was later to describe Reilly as "a man of indomitable courage, a genius as an agent but a sinister man whom I could never bring myself wholly to trust." However, Cumming was to remain tolerant of Reilly's antics for some three to four years. In September 1920, when Naval Intelligence complained that Reilly was going about Paris in a British naval uniform, C brushed this aside with the comment that he "is employed by me and is engaged at present on a highly important and confidential mission."

In light of what was to pass, Reilly's remit in Russia in spring 1918 is important. C apparently sent him on a limited, three-month stint to keep tabs on military affairs, as a "military agent."

Reilly himself said later that his "instructions were to counter, as far as possible, the work being done by the German agents [in Russia], and to report on the general feeling in the Russian capital." But more specifically, like the rest of the British intelligence establishment in Russia in spring-summer 1918, Reilly was charged with assisting in the effort to keep Allied military stockpiles, supplied to the tsar's army during the world war and stored mainly in the northern ports of Arkhangelsk and Murmansk, and the Russian navy, primarily its Baltic squadron, out of German and, subsequently, Bolshevik hands.

But Reilly was soon to involve himself in brutal high politics—trying nothing less than to engineer the overthrow of the Bolshevik government. MI6 was later to imply that this change in Reilly's mandate was due to the influence of R. H. B. Lockhart, London's political agent in Moscow in 1918, who used their man for a "political purpose." Reilly, according to MI6, had specifically been warned by his superiors "that he was not . . . to get mixed up with politics." But this institutional denial may have been merely pro forma. There is really no knowing whether C or someone else in London had given Reilly a green (or perhaps yellow) light for something more far-reaching than collecting intelligence. Certainly from the start, Reilly, in Petrograd and Moscow, acted as if his remit went well beyond information gathering.

As things turned out, MI6 had sent Reilly off to Moscow much as German intelligence had sent off Lenin, in his sealed car, from Switzerland to the Finland Station, Petrograd, the previous year: to topple an inimical regime. But the Germans had been successful; MI6, with Reilly, was not.

In Southampton, Reilly boarded the Danish merchantman the *Queen Mary*, bound for Arkhangelsk. On March 29, 1918, C cabled the British legation in Vologda, north of Moscow—to which the Western embassies had moved the previous month from Petrograd, fearing the advancing German army—that

Reilly was on his way: "[He] carries code message of identification . . . Ask him what his business is and he will answer 'Diamond buying' . . . He will be at your disposal, utilize him to join up your organization if necessary as he should travel freely. Return him to Stockholm end of June."

But Reilly, contrary to instructions, disembarked at Murmansk, before the ship reached Arkhangelsk, and was immediately arrested by the British military, who controlled the port. His passport was problematic. It bore the name "Reilli"—and "he was obviously not an Irishman," recalled the local MI6 officer Stephen Alley. (Alley, known as "Sally," was born in Moscow, the son of a British railway expert who worked in Russia. Alley was recruited by Cumming at the start of World War One and for a time was responsible for SIS operations in the vast territory comprising Russia, Finland, Estonia, Latvia, and Romania. After the war, Alley moved to MI5, where he stayed until the end of World War Two.) When Reilly produced a "microscopic coded message" hidden in a bottle of aspirin, however, he was immediately released. He then made tracks for Petrograd, which, he recalled later, "bore a ruinous and tumbledown aspect. The streets were dirty, reeking, squalid . . . strewn with litter and garbage. There was no police except for the secret police . . . no municipal administration, no sanitary arrangements, no shops open, no busy passengers on the pavements, no hustle of traffic on the roads. The place had sunk into utter stagnation. . . . The bread queues [he had already encountered in 1915] were still there, but [now] there was no food at all. The great mass of the people was starving."

On April 16, he reported to C from Petrograd: the Bolsheviks, he said, were the "only real power" in Russia, but the opposition was "constantly growing and if suitably supported will finally lead to overthrow of the Bolsheviks." Clearly, Reilly's mind was toying with something beyond intelligence gathering. He asked for "one million pounds" to bolster the anti-Bolshevik movement, insisting that the moment was "critical"—immediate action was necessary, or else all hope of overthrowing the Bolsheviks must be abandoned. In the short term, Reilly wrote, the aim should be to secure Arkhangelsk and Murmansk and to keep out of Bolshevik hands the "enormous quantities of metals, ammunition and artillery" stockpiled in the two ports and to prevent the Russian Baltic fleet from falling into German hands. In the longer term, Reilly was advocating the overthrow of the revolutionary regime. Indeed, he seemed to be inching toward the role of counterrevolutionary orchestrator.

Reilly's resolve may have been reinforced by a speech delivered in Petrograd on April 28 by the new war commissar (appointed in mid-March), Leon Trotsky, which he attended. Trotsky spoke of the impending "doom of the ruling classes" and, according to ST1's report, advocated "merciless class war." Trotsky said that Russia's "territorial losses" to Germany and the Whites (see below) would be reversed with the advent of the "International Proletarian Revolution." According to Reilly, the audience understood the speech as he did—it was a "shrewd prevarications of facts [*sic*], insinuating misconstruction . . . and a lack of inner conviction . . . hammering reiteration, stridency of voice and clutching gestures [that] served as substitutes [for the truth?]." "Not more than one half [of the audience] applauded at any time," Reilly reported. (Clearly Reilly was shortchanging Trotsky, who by most accounts was a brilliant and mesmerizing orator.) One source has it that Reilly, who sat a stone's throw away from the speaker, had muttered under his breath, "This is just the moment to kill Trotsky and liquidate Bolshevism!"

Raymond Robins, head of the American Red Cross mission in Petrograd, said that "Trotsky was [a] poor kind [of] son of a bitch but [the] greatest Jew since Christ." The identification of Bolshevism with Jewry at this time was common among Westerners involved in Russian affairs, mainly because of the profusion of Jews in the Bolshevik leadership. General Edmund Ironside, the commander of the Allied intervention force in northern Russia the following year, as he assumed his position issued a "proclamation" to his troops that stated: "Look at Russia at the present moment. The power is in the hands of a few men, mostly Jews, who have succeeded in bringing the country to such a state that order is non-existent. . . . Every man who wants something . . . just kills his opponent, only to be killed himself when the next man comes along. . . . Bolshevism is a disease which, like consumption, kills its victim and brings no good to anybody." (Ironside was immediately reined in by the Foreign Office, which regarded the "proclamation" as inappropriate. He was instructed henceforward to vet his proclamations with the foreign and war offices.)

Reilly arrived in Moscow a few days later. "The new masters," he reported, "were exercising a regime of bloodthirstiness and horror hardly equaled in history. The most ignorant and the most vile . . . were in the ascendancy." Russia, according to Reilly's friend Alexander "Sasha" Grammatikoff, a former Okhrana agent and, later, a Reilly business associate, was "in the hands of the criminal classes and of lunatics released from the asylums." The Bolsheviks, in control of Russia's power centers, were out to "master every country in the world." Bolshevism, Reilly told London, was "a hideous cancer striking at the very root of civilization."

On May 7, displaying outlandish chutzpah, Reilly showed up, in full RFC regalia, at the gates of the Kremlin, demanding to see Lenin. He said that he had previously met with General Mikhail Dmitriyevich Bonch-Bruevich, the military director of the Supreme Military Council, an advisor to Trotsky, and his deputy, Nikolai Ilyich Podvoisky. Mikhail, incidentally, was the brother of Vladimir Bonch-Bruevich, Lenin's private secretary. Reilly demanded to see the leader himself, saying he was a personal emissary from Lloyd George (it is just possible that, accompanied by C, Reilly had actually met with the prime minister before leaving London) and wished "to obtain first-hand news of the aims and ideals of the Bolsheviks." The flummoxed Kremlin officials rang the newly installed British representative in Moscow, Lockhart, to query Reilly's bona fides.

Lockhart was one of those ill-fitting mavericks who every so often spring into the limelight from the midst of the staid British establishment. He came from a mix of Scottish Highlands clans ("there is no drop of English blood in my veins") and, in his youth, excelled in rugby. He had "a genius for drifting," as he put it in his best-selling autobiography, *Memoirs of a British Agent* (1932), and after high school, instead of going up to Cambridge, moved to Berlin and then Paris for three years, mastering German and French. Then he sailed east, to Malaya, and ran a rubber plantation. He contracted malaria, which he was to suffer from periodically throughout his life; fell head over heels for a local beauty and cohabited with her, to the locals' chagrin; and was extricated in the nick of time by his family and the British authorities. Back in Britain, he passed the consular service exam and, in 1912, was posted to Moscow as vice consul. In September 1917, after serving for two years as acting consul-general and befriending several of the moderate socialists who had overthrown the tsar in February, he was gently persuaded by his boss, the British ambassador, to leave the country due to his sticky romance with a "Russian Jewess." He missed being on the spot during the October Revolution by two months.

Lockhart's attitude toward the Russian revolutions and revolutionaries of 1917–1918 combined a degree of sympathy for their ideals, vision, and courage with *realpolitik* considerations of benefit to Britain. Back in London in late 1917, he lobbied vigorously for the establishment of relations with the new, Bolshevik regime. Many Britons were horrified by the assumption of power by the revolutionaries, who openly preached "world revolution." "I argued that it was madness not to establish some contact with the men who at that moment were controlling Russia's destinies," Lockhart recalled.

In mid-1917, during his last months in Russia, Lockhart was persuaded that the moderate socialists led by Kerensky, who had assumed power in February, couldn't prevail and that the Bolsheviks would soon take over as they were the only party with real popular support. The Bolshevik message—peace, meaning an end to Russian participation in the war, and bread and land, meaning a redistribution of wealth, including the transfer of agricultural holdings to the peasantry—trumped anything the monarchist, moderate socialist, or liberal bourgeois parties were offering.

Prime Minister Lloyd George was at least partly persuaded and, egged on by War Cabinet member Lord Milner, who had become Lockhart's patron, in January 1918 appointed Lockhart as "agent" or head of delegation to the Bolshevik government, an unofficial diplomatic posting and mission. (As a quid pro quo, the British agreed that Maxim Litvinov would be officially recognized as the representative of the Bolshevik regime in London.) The prime minister hoped that Lockhart could persuade the Bolsheviks to reverse their stance on the war or at least disrupt a Russian-German detente. Lockhart arrived in Petrograd on January 30, 1918, and moved to Moscow around March 20, days after the Bolshevik government reached the city, having abandoned Petrograd for fear of an impending German onslaught and conquest. The Germans never came—but the Soviet government remained in Moscow.

In the months following the Bolshevik takeover, Western governments began to weigh sending military forces to Russia. Some Western leaders feared that, with the breakdown and withdrawal from the front of the Russian army, Germany might seek to push eastward and conquer parts or all of European Russia, laying hold of Russia's armaments, ammunition stockpiles, and raw materials, which would strengthen Germany, against whom their armies were still fighting along the French frontier (World War One was to end only in early November 1918). On December 2, 1917, months before they signed the Brest-Litovsk peace treaty, Russia and Germany agreed to an armistice, and in mid-February 1918 German forces thrust eastward in "Operation Thunderbolt," taking Minsk (February 21), Kiev (March 2), Narva (March 4), Odessa (March 14), Kharkov (April 8), Sevastopol (May 1), and Rostov (May 8). The Allies worried that the Germans would push still farther east and perhaps coerce the Russians into aligning with them.

But Western military intervention was not contemplated only as a foil against German expansionism and empowerment. From the first, the idea was tinged with an anti-Bolshevik undertone, at least in London. From early 1917 it was clear that the Bolsheviks were bent on taking Russia out of the war, which would severely weaken the Allied cause. And the Bolshevik assumption of power in November immediately touched off a civil war between the gradually mobilizing White and Red Russian forces, a civil war that only ended, with Bolshevik victory, in 1923. The Whites consisted mainly of remnants of the tsarist ancien régime, much of the old army's officer corps, and the Cossack bands of southern and central Russia.

The Western powers (and Japan) gradually inched toward supporting the Whites. Already on December 3, 1917, the British War Cabinet, "after some hesitation," had decided to supply funds to movements in Russia that were "anti-Bolshevik and pro-Entente," and pledged "unlimited British financial aid" to the anti-Bolshevik Cossack ataman (chief) in the Don region, General A. M. Kaledin. Then, three weeks later, the British and French prime ministers agreed to "do everything we could to support the [anti-Bolshevik] movements in the South and South-east of Russia, and elsewhere if they should develop, and it was distinctly agreed that if the result of such action was to produce a rupture with the Bolsheviks we should not be deterred by that happening." During the following months, British pledges of support were also given to the White general Michael Vassilevich Alexeyev, the former chief of staff of the tsar's army who at the end of 1917 had founded the Volunteer Army, and to his deputies, the ex-tsarist generals Lavr Kornilov and Anton Denikin, who had risen against the Bolsheviks in the Kuban region.

Toward the end of 1917 and during early 1918 additional anti-Bolshevik White and nationalist armies had consolidated west, north, and east of Moscow. But as Trotsky noted, the British for months remained undecided about whom exactly to support or whether to intervene militarily or sit out the unfolding civil war. Russia was vast and the Allies were still heavily engaged in Flanders Fields, and their publics were reluctant to embark on additional, ideologically controversial adventures. "Your Lloyd George is like a man playing roulette and scattering chips on every number," Trotsky, now commissar for war, was quoted as saying.

But the British, from the first, were forthright and clear about one thing: war materials and armaments, especially the Russian fleets in the Baltic and Black Seas, must not fall into German hands. In June 1918, the Russian Black Sea fleet, based at Novorossiysk and Sevastopol, was scuttled by its crews after receiving financial inducements from Allied intelligence officers.

The Russian civil war had already begun, in effect, on November 10, 1917, when young officer-cadets rose against the Bolsheviks inside Petrograd as Cossack units under General P. N. Krasnov attempted to push into the city from outside. Armed workers and soldiers of the city's soviet (a workers and soldiers council) suppressed the rebellion and drove back Krasnov's forces. During the following months the Bolshevik government projected its power, based on local urban soviets in the core Russian area, northward, eastward, and southward, from the Polish border to the Pacific. But they were initially unsuccessful in quashing the Cossack hosts in the Don, Kuban, and Terek regions of the south, or in the Ukraine, or in the Baltic area, where the local peoples—Finns, Latvians, Lithuanians, and Estonians—mounted a protracted and ultimately successful resistance. Most of Siberia, too, remained out of Red control for some two years.

In the south, where the Soviets took Rostov on February 24, 1918, the Cossacks, alongside the Volunteer Army, surged back in the spring, aided by Germany's February–May offensive into the Ukraine and Don areas (the Germans entered Rostov-on-Don on May 8; the Don Cossacks ejected the Reds from their capital Novocherkassk on May 6). The Cossacks failed to take Tsaritsyn (renamed Stalingrad in 1925). But by mid-1918, after recovering from initial reverses, the Whites in the south briefly threatened the Bolshevik heartland. By the end of August 1918, the Volunteer Army, now numbering 30,000, had driven the Bolsheviks out of the whole of Kuban, taking Novorossiysk on the 26th. A mixed British-French naval force arrived in Novorossiysk at the end of November, bringing French and British military missions to Denikin's new HQ at Ekaterinodar (after 1920, Krasnodar). In December 1918, a French force of 1,800 colonial troops landed in Odessa. While failing to take Moscow, the southern White forces continued to hold their own in the core Don-Kuban region and proved the most serious civil war threat to Bolshevik power. The Red Army only vanquished them there in the spring of 1920.

To the east, from spring 1918 the Reds faced three challenges: an invading Japanese army; the "Czech Legion" splayed out between the Pacific and the Urals, along the line of the Trans-Siberian Railway; and Admiral Alexander Kolchak's White Army, based in Omsk.

The Japanese expeditionary army, with 70,000 troops at its height, occupied Vladivostok and other Russian Pacific Rim towns starting April 4, 1918, after Russian troops killed some local Japanese shopkeepers. During the following years, there were infrequent clashes between the Japanese invaders and Red units. The last Japanese troops left Russian territory—Sakhalin and Kamchatka—in 1925.

The more serious threat in the east were the two Czech divisions, made up mostly of Russian-captured Habsburg troops gradually assembled and organized by Allied officers during 1914–1918 as an auxiliary force assisting the tsar's fight against the Austro-Hungarian army. Following Brest-Litovsk, the Czech legionnaires wanted to repatriate. But the Red Army blocked their passage eastward and threatened to disarm them. Trotsky even announced that "every armed Czechoslovak found on the railway is to be shot on the spot." On May 25, 1918, the Czech regiments revolted, seizing key points along the Trans-Siberian Railway line. On June 29, Czech units entered Vladivostok, hoping to board ships to carry them back to Europe via the Pacific. But nothing materialized, and for two years, starting in the summer of 1918, the Czech Legion, now numbering some 60,000 soldiers and supported by the Allied governments, periodically fought the Red Army and hesitantly supported Kolchak's White forces. But his British-equipped "Provisional All-Russian Government" never attained control of all of Siberia, let alone of the White camp generally, and finally disintegrated at the start of 1920; Red troops executed him in February. The Reds subsequently agreed to allow the Czechs to depart, and by September all had sailed out of Vladivostok. Months later, after a circuitous journey, they reached the newly established Republic of Czechoslovakia, where they formed the core of the new state's army.

In the north, British troops occupied Murmansk on March 6, 1918, and, supported by 2,000 French soldiers, landed at Arkhangelsk on August 1–2, in parallel with a revolt by local Whites who ousted the region's Bolshevik regime. By February

1919 there were 18,000 Allied troops in Arkhangelsk, one-third of them British, and 16,000 in Murmansk, most of them British. Everyone expected the Allied force to march southward, to Vologda, and from there perhaps on toward Moscow. But the feelers General Poole sent out stopped after seventy miles; his force was too small to attempt a grand anti-Bolshevik intervention to capture Petrograd and Moscow.

Initially, Lockhart had opposed Western military intervention. Days after the signing of the German-Soviet Brest-Litovsk peace treaty on March 3, 1918, Lockhart, now back in Moscow, cabled London: "The humiliating peace is the beginning of a national revival in Russia. . . . The Bolsheviks may help in this revival. . . . They may simply be the nucleus of a real national resistance [to the Germans]. . . . It should be our business to foster this revival whatever form it should take. . . . The peace . . . is the beginning of a strong Russia." He also advised London that "our great danger at present is counter-revolution. . . . Counter-revolution at present would be fatal to Allied interests here . . . I feel most strongly that we should support [Trotsky] in every way."

Lockhart was severely rebuked by anti-Bolshevik "interventionists" such as Major-General Alfred Knox, head of the British military mission in Siberia, and Lord Hardinge, the permanent undersecretary of state at the Foreign Office. Knox: "Lockhart . . . proposes to play with the Bolsheviks. He was already deeply entangled in their webs but the worst of it is that he continued persistently to buzz and people here listened to his buzzing." Hardinge: "All his forecasts have proved wrong. . . . He is hysterical and has achieved nothing."

Lockhart quickly understood that he was swimming against the current, with fellow Allied officials, especially the French, and the British military mission officers in Russia, including Major-General Frederick Cuthbert Poole in Arkhangelsk, the commander-in-chief of Allied forces in northern Russia, forcefully advocating military intervention to topple the Bolshevik regime or, at least, to prevent a German-Russian rapprochement. Foreign Secretary Balfour himself rebuked Lockhart: "You have at different times advised against Allied intervention in any form; against it by the Japanese alone; against it with Japanese assistance; against it at Vladivostok; in favour of it at Murmansk; in favour of it with an [Bolshevik] invitation; in favour of it without an invitation. . . . In favour of it without invitation whether the Bolsheviks desired it or not."

But Brest-Litovsk proved the clincher. The Soviet government had definitively abandoned the Allies and the war, and Lockhart now worried that the Russians and Germans were inching toward cooperation that would necessarily harm Allied interests. By May 1918, Lockhart had joined the advocates of intervention, at least to the extent of supporting an intervention designed to prevent German dominance of European Russia. In a cable to London on May 26 he described a conversation he had had with "one of [Boris] Savinkof's agents . . . Savinkof's plans for counter-revolution are based entirely on Allied intervention. The French Mission [to Russia] has been supporting them and has assured [Savinkov, a counterrevolutionary leader] that intervention is already decided. Savinkof proposes to murder all Bolshevik leaders on night of Allies landing and to form a Government which will be in reality a military dictatorship." Lockhart appeared to endorse Savinkov's demand for "immediate action."

By winter, after his failure in the summer to overthrow the Bolshevik regime (see below) and his return to London, Lockhart became a staunch advocate of aggressive Allied military intervention. He wrote Balfour that "Allied intervention would seem to be the most important need of the moment. . . . Our intervention is justified on humanitarian grounds, and . . . we should do more by proceeding openly against the Bolsheviks than by trying to suppress them surreptitiously." Reflecting on the events of the previous months, he wrote: "I am of the opinion that had we been in a position, after the Czecho-Slovak outbreak [the Czech Legion's rebellion of May–June 1918], to land two divisions at Archangel, together with an American-Japanese force in Siberia, the Bolsheviks might easily have collapsed."

(However, in his memoirs published in 1932, Lockhart repented and bemoaned his pro-interventionist *volte face*, writing: "[For the Allies] to have intervened at all was a mistake. To have intervened with hopelessly inadequate forces [i.e., incapable of actually crushing the Bolsheviks] was an example of spineless half-measures which, in the circumstances, amounted to a crime." He was, of course, referring to the British landing in Arkhangelsk in August 1918, which had frightened and angered the Bolsheviks without actually affecting the balance of power; neither did it stop Germany's march eastward or force Germany to siphon off troops to Russia from the Western Front, where the Allies were being pressed hard by the Germans' last offensive of the world war.)

Such was the regional and international backdrop to Reilly's activities in Russia in the spring and summer of 1918. On May 7, as we have seen, Kremlin officials had telephoned Lockhart and said that a man in British military uniform calling himself "Relli" had shown up at the gate and, claiming he had been sent by Lloyd George, demanded to see Lenin. (Surprisingly, he was admitted and got as far as Vladimir Bonch-Bruevich, Lenin's secretary.)

The officials summoned Lockhart and asked him whether "Relli" was an "imposter." Lockhart later recorded that he was "nonplussed" and "nearly blurted out that he must be a Russian masquerading as an Englishman or else a madman." But, adopting caution, he said he would check. He contacted Ernest Boyce, head of SIS in Moscow. Boyce told him that Reilly was, indeed, "a new [SIS] agent." Lockhart recorded that he "blew up in a storm of indignation. . . . The sheer audacity of the man took my breath away."

That day or the next, Lockhart met Reilly for the first time. Lockhart recorded: "Although he was years older than me, I dressed him down like a schoolmaster and threatened to have him sent home. He took his wigging humbly but calmly and was so ingenious in his excuses that in the end he made me laugh."

But talk of sending him back to London, as some of Lockhart's aides advised, was empty bluster. Reilly was C's current blue-eyed boy. As the director of military intelligence in London made clear to the head of the British military mission in Murmansk-Arkhangelsk at the time, Reilly (and a fellow SIS officer, "Lt. Mitchelson") were "engaged on special secret service." Lockhart later summarized: "The man who had thrust himself so dramatically into my life was Sidney Reilly, the mystery man of the British secret service and known to-day [1932] to the outside world as the master spy of Britain." Secret service work might not amount to much, Lockhart opined, but "the methods of Sidney Reilly . . . were on a grand scale, which compelled my admiration." Lockhart went on to describe Reilly as "by far the cleverest of our agents in Russia."

His bona fides confirmed, Reilly set about establishing connections with the Bolshevik military leadership—just as Trotsky was busy putting together the Red Army to counter the White threat. This new army was based on the militiamen of the workers councils (the soviets), leavened with a large number of turncoat ex-tsarist officers. Like Lockhart, Reilly quickly grasped that with energetic, intelligent leadership such as Trotsky's, the Bolsheviks would soon have a powerful military instrument—contrary to the skeptical view of the heads of the British military mission, as conveyed in the reports to London by Colonel C. J. M. Thornhill, the head of British military intelligence in Russia.

ST1 immediately established a firm relationship with General Mikhail Bonch-Bruevich ("BB"), Vladimir's brother and military director of the Supreme Military Council—effectively, Trotsky's deputy. They were to meet repeatedly during the following weeks, as Reilly reported to London. BB probably saw Reilly as a source of information about British thinking or, at least, as a channel to the British government. For Reilly, BB was a source of intelligence on the Bolshevik military. Reilly described BB as "a student" (i.e., scholar) rather than "a man of action." The Bolsheviks, he reported in mid-May, were now adopting "a more rational and common sense outlook"—meaning that they sought cooperation with the Western Allies against the Germans. At least, that was what BB led Reilly to believe.

Perhaps this was an accurate reflection of BB's (and Trotsky's) views. BB, like most of the revolutionary leadership, certainly sought Allied recognition of the Bolshevik government. He told Reilly that he had the agreement of both Lenin and Trotsky to supply the Allies "with all military intelligence." Apparently BB was referring to what the Russians knew of German capabilities, intentions, and operations. Indeed, BB went so far as to say that he favored a "rising"—meaning renewal of the war—against the German occupiers on Russian soil. In early June, while Reilly was in BB's office, Trotsky called and approved BB's proposal for a proclamation to this effect. The Reilly-BB exchanges took place after the signing of the Brest-Litovsk pact and the German invasion of Russia's western marchlands, Ukraine and the Baltic provinces. Many Bolsheviks, including BB, and perhaps Trotsky as well, came to believe that, at Brest-Litovsk, Russia had conceded too much, with imminent German conquest of Petrograd, and perhaps even Moscow, a possible outcome.

But Lenin and acting (later permanent) foreign affairs commissar Georgy Chicherin favored strict adherence to Brest-Litovsk, whatever Germany's infringements, and even agreed to new German demands, such as "the cession to Finland of West Murman," Finnish or German control of the Rybachi Peninsula, and removal of the remainder of the Black Sea fleet to German-occupied Sebastopol from Novorossiysk. BB argued: "Cannot the Allies see that by keeping aloof [i.e., not recognizing the Bolshevik government], they give a free hand to Germany, that they are abandoning us. . . . If they wait much longer there will be no Russia to save."

But BB may have been playing a double game. While he was passing conciliatory messages to London via Reilly, other Bolshevik officials, guided by Lenin, were secretly negotiating a new political and economic agreement with Berlin that would grant Germany new concessions. The Germans were promised oil from Baku and, in exchange, had apparently agreed to help the Bolsheviks drive the British out of Vologda. A secret agreement to this effect was signed in Berlin on August 27.

But Reilly's attitude toward the Bolsheviks was deeply felt and unwavering, and unaffected by momentary diplomatic posturing. From the start, he was bent on overthrowing Bolshevik rule—a sentiment in line with mainstream British government wishes if not concrete policy. After his meetings with BB, Reilly shed his RFC uniform and went underground. Perhaps he added or shed facial hairs as well (we don't know which). He now called himself "Mr. Constantine," a Greek businessman, or "Konstantin Markovich Massino," a Turkish merchant, and shuttled between Moscow and Petrograd. In Moscow, he took up residence at 3 Sheremet'evski Lane, a flat rented by Elizaveta Emilyevna Otten, a twenty-two-year-old blonde German actress, and Dagmara Karozus, a dancer at the Moscow Arts Theater. Reilly appears to have slept with both of them, separately or together. In Petrograd, which he visited regularly, he shared an apartment with Elena Mikhailovna Boyuzhovskaya at 10 Torgovaya Street. He also established a third identity, for which he had Bolshevik regime papers in the name of "Sigmund Rellinsky," of the Cheka's criminal investigation department, arranged for him by the secret anti-Bolshevik Vladimir Orlov, a Cheka officer who had served in Russian military intelligence during World War One.

The Cheka—or All-Russian Extraordinary Commission for Combating Counter-Revolution, Profiteering, and Corruption, the Bolsheviks' secret (political) police—was founded in December 1917 by Felix Edmunovich Dzerzhinsky, son of a minor Polish nobleman. He was described by sculptor Clare Sheridan, who created a likeness of him in 1920, as "calm and sphinx-like. . . . A deep cough periodically shook his body and forced the blood up to his face." He was a fanatical Communist (though in his youth, like Stalin, he had hoped to become a priest). In its first months, the Cheka consisted of some forty officers, backed by several companies of regular Red Army troops. During the civil war, the Cheka expanded exponentially and by 1920 had 200,000 employees.

During May–July 1918 Reilly set about organizing a counterrevolution to topple the Bolshevik regime while assisting Allied intervention in Russia's hinterlands. With both ends in mind, Reilly hoped to make use of allegedly disaffected Latvian (Lettish) units, which at the time were the elite formations of the Red Army and served as a type of Praetorian Guard in Moscow. Reilly was later to compare himself to the "Corsican lieutenant" who had emerged as France's emperor in the wake of the 1789 revolution: "Surely a British espionage agent . . . could make himself master of Moscow?" he was quoted as saying. Reilly made contact with disaffected Russian officers and officials; helped MI6's Captain George Alexander Hill set up a courier service for clandestine messages and intelligence reports; rented and organized safe houses; and recruited agents who, aside from intelligence collection, could serve as saboteurs of regime targets. Hill, saying Reilly "knew the situation better than any other British officer in Russia," left "the political control [of the network] and our policy [?] in his hands."

Curiously, Reilly at this time also suggested to Whitehall an alternative, or complementary, strategy for overthrowing Bolshevism—through religion. In June 1918 he proposed that the Allies finance a large-scale religious program which would involve setting up a network of "church schools all over Russia," reinforced by "the widest participation of the clergy in educational work outside the schools and the church." The villages, he wrote, should be flooded "with appropriate literature" and there should be a campaign of "personal spiritual propaganda and agitation over the whole country." All of this would result in "imperishable ties between the Russian people and the [Christian] Allied nations." Reilly estimated that the cost would be "20–25 million" rubles. How seriously Reilly took this idea— he proposed it only the once—we don't really know. But it was apparently arranged with Lockhart, who, it was reported— perhaps with exaggeration concerning the amount—raised some "12 million rubles" and handed them to Reilly, which Reilly and Hill then handed over to the Russian church patriarch Tikhon. What specifically the money was meant to do or what the patriarch subsequently did with it we don't know.

Meanwhile, anti-Bolshevik Russians independently stepped up their militant activities, such as attacking Bolshevik officials, throwing Russia into political turmoil. These uncontrolled operations, as we shall see, ultimately helped undermine the preparations by Reilly and the Allies for their own *coup de main*.

The first attack came on June 20, 1918, when gunmen assassinated Moisei Goldstein Volodarsky, the Bolshevik commissar for press affairs in Petrograd. Then came the full-blown Left Socialist Revolutionary Party operation of July 6, the third day of the Fifth All-Russian Congress at the Moscow Opera House, a convention of moderate socialist and Bolshevik leaders from around the country. The operation amounted to an attempted coup d'état. The Left SR—a breakaway from the Kerensky-supporting mainstream of the Socialist Revolutionary Party—were, since November 1917, members of the Lenin-led coalition government. But they disagreed with the Bolsheviks over the discontinuation of the war against Germany and finally broke with them over Brest-Litovsk.

The Left SR plot had three prongs: to assassinate the German ambassador in Moscow, possibly reigniting the Russo-German war; to take over key installations in the Bolshevik capital; and to capture a swath of territory in Moscow's outskirts, perhaps with the ultimate aim of marching on Moscow itself.

A team of assassins, posing as Cheka officers ostensibly intent on warning the new German ambassador, Count Wilhelm von Mirbach, that there was a plot afoot to kill him, gained entry into the German embassy. When the count asked them how the assassins proposed to carry out their plan, the gunman, Yakov Bliumkin, drew his Browning pistol and shouted, "Like this!" and emptied it into the ambassador. He then hurled a grenade and jumped out the window. Meanwhile, Left SR troops briefly took control of a number of buildings in the capital, including the telephone and telegraph exchange, and arrested Dzerzhinsky, the head of the Cheka, who had come to Left SR headquarters to head off the rebellion. They then advanced on the opera house, only to be deterred by the strong Bolshevik armed presence. Trotsky then rallied the two Lettish regiments in the capital and rounded up the rebels. It was all over within hours.

As the shooting unfolded outside the opera house, Reilly, who was attending the congress as an observer, had a close call. Fearing a Bolshevik search, he tore up and swallowed some of the subversive documents on his person (possibly linking him or the Allies to the SR plot).

Simultaneously with the Mirbach assassination and the lunge at the opera house, Boris Savinkov, the veteran terrorist who headed the SR's military wing and former deputy war minister in Kerensky's government, with several hundred fighters at his beck, took control of Yaroslavl, a small town northwest of the capital on the road to Vologda, and issued a general call to rebellion, triggering minor revolts in Rybinsk and Murom. Already three months before, in late April 1918, Savinkov, with British intelligence funding, had tried to organize a coup, but the Cheka, getting wind of the plot, had headed it off. Now, in July, Savinkov tried again—and again he failed. Again, too, he appears to have been funded by the British, as Lockhart later confessed ("Bountiful promises of men and money were held out"). It appears he believed that Allied forces were about to land in Arkhangelsk, with whom he hoped to link up.

For two weeks the Bolsheviks bombarded Yaroslavl with artillery and from the air. The revolt collapsed and Savinkov fled to central Europe. The Left SR had hoped to overturn the Brest-Litovsk agreement, if not actually take over the government.

For the following six years, Savinkov was the most prominent counterrevolutionary Russian outside Russia and the leader of the dispersed "movement" of the left-of-center exiles and their supporters inside Russia, an activist, a figurehead, and an inspiration—until his apprehension and execution by the Cheka (or OGPU, as it was known after 1922). Somerset Maugham, the British spy and, later, playwright and novelist, described Savinkov as "the most remarkable man I met [in Russia?]." But not everyone was taken with Savinkov. George Hill described him as "a morphine addict and a coward." Before 1917, when Savinkov was a leading anti-tsarist conspirator, "he organized thirty-three assassination plots but never dared [to] throw a bomb himself."

Churchill met Savinkov in 1921 and was completely won over. At base they shared having had adventure-packed youths, as well as an antipathy toward Bolshevism. Churchill said, "Of all the tyrannies in history, the Bolshevist tyranny is the worst, the most destructive, and the most degrading." After Savinkov died, Churchill included him (alongside George Bernard Shaw, Lord Curzon, Lawrence of Arabia, and Hitler) in his 1932 volume of portraits of "great contemporaries," and recalled: "I had never seen a Russian Nihilist except on the stage and my first impression was that he was singularly well cast for the part. Small in stature; moving as little as possible, and that noiselessly and with deliberation; remarkably grey-green eyes in a face of almost deadly pallor; speaking in a calm, low, even voice, almost a monotone; innumerable cigarettes . . . " Churchill called him a "terrorist" with "moderate aims."

After 1917, Churchill and Savinkov were on the same (anti-Bolshevik) side and Churchill forgave him his youthful excesses. Indeed, he was so enthused that in 1921, after Reilly underhandedly obtained a British entry visa for Savinkov, Churchill took Savinkov to Chequers, the prime ministerial retreat in Buckinghamshire, to meet Lloyd George. According to Savinkov, the prime minister and his family sang along with him "God Save the Tsar." Afterward, the two men talked. But the prime minister, unlike Churchill, was not persuaded at that point to back counterrevolution in Russia; instead he argued that either the Bolshevik leaders would gradually become moderate or they would be devoured by their own, much as Robespierre and Saint-Just had been in the French Revolution.

The victor of the battle for Yaroslavl was Trotsky, who had become, almost overnight, a highly efficient and resolute war commissar, serially crushing the Bolsheviks' opponents. He was to go on to win the unfolding civil war against the Whites. Lockhart, who knew Trotsky, described him as brilliant, "all temperament, an individualist and an artist" (in contrast with Lenin, who was cold, "impersonal and almost inhuman"). Curiously, Lockhart, in his memoirs, was to compare Trotsky to Shimon

Bar Kokhba, the Judean rebel who rose against the Romans in AD 132 and (apparently) conquered Jerusalem, for a while holding the Romans at bay, until he died in the Roman assault on his last stronghold, Beitar, in AD 135.

The crushing of the Left SR rebellion strengthened the Bolsheviks' hold on power, but also reinforced their wariness of counterrevolutionary plotting in general. At the same time, the rebellion energized Reilly and Lockhart to press forward with their own conspiratorial plans. Indeed, at the opera house during the revolutionaries' congress Reilly had even managed to pick up a twenty-five-year-old secretary, Olga Dmitrievna Starzhevskaya, who worked in a key government office. They quickly became lovers—and she, of course, became one of his agents. He gave her 20,000 rubles and she set up yet another safe house in Moscow. (It was not an inconsiderable sum. At the time, a cab ride cost 100 rubles, and a pair of boots 800 rubles.)

Gradually, the Reilly Plot (which many historians subsequently called the Ambassadors' Plot or the Lockhart Plot) matured, but under the watchful eye of the Cheka, who, from late June 1918, seem to have tracked much of the Reilly-Lockhart operation. Although Lockhart may have written that the Cheka "was terrifying but far from clever," in fact they proved quite efficient, serially uncovering and closing down opposition groups—albeit usually killing and arresting many innocents and the partially innocent as well as the guilty along the way.

Hill was later to describe the plot—in which he himself played a major part—as "bold and masterfully conceived." Reilly made contact with old pals from the tsarist army and administration and roped in officials and officers from the Kerensky regime, liberals and socialists. He even drew up a shadow cabinet that would replace the Bolshevik ministers—including General Nikolai Yudenich (war minister), Alexander Grammatikoff (interior minister), and Vladimir Orlov (justice). Added impetus was given to the plotters when news arrived that Tsar Nicholas and his family had been murdered on July 17 by Bolsheviks in Ekaterinburg and that the two-division-strong Czech Legion east of Moscow was (supposedly) advancing on the capital. On July 27, 1918, the Allied embassies moved from Vologda—where they had been since February, having decamped from Petrograd— to Arkhangelsk in advance of the Allied landing at the port, which all believed was coming. Three days later, in Kiev, a young Russian student assassinated the commander-in-chief of the German forces in Russia, General Hermann von Eichhorn.

But already in June, the heads of the Cheka, Dzerzhinsky and his deputy, Jacob (Yakov) Peters, sensing the brewing Western intervention and the local counterrevolutionary plotting, and suspecting a potential nexus between the two, launched what amounted to a counterplot. They sent two newly recruited Cheka operatives, former Latvian junior officers Jan Buikis and Jan Sprogis, calling themselves respectively Shmidkhen and Bredis, to sniff around in Petrograd. Posing as disaffected Bolsheviks, they hung around the Lettish Club, a watering hole and entertainment center opposite the Russian Admiralty building where British naval officers occasionally came to drink and dance. One of these Britons was Captain Francis Cromie, a submarine commander who had just been appointed British naval attaché, with offices in the (Petrograd) British embassy building (the actual embassy had already moved to Vologda). But he was no diplomat. He once wrote, "A Russian only understands a big stick and a big threat, anything else is taken for weakness. One must not forget that one is not dealing with a European, but with a cunning and cruel savage." Waitresses at the club described Cromie as "a serious man" who preferred talking to dancing. The two Letts eventually struck up a conversation with him, pretending that they were anti-Bolsheviks. At a follow-up meeting at a nearby hotel they discussed possible plans. Cromie then introduced the two to Reilly, who proposed that the Letts travel to Moscow and meet Lockhart.

A few days later, in early August, the two showed up at Lockhart's flat. They introduced themselves as Latvian counterrevolutionaries and claimed that there were many disaffected Latvian soldiers who, like themselves, sought Latvian independence, not a Communist restructuring of society. Lockhart took the bait and issued them passes with which they could make their way unimpeded to British lines at Arkhangelsk, to prepare the ground for cooperation between the Brits and the Latvian units that would head north from Moscow, ostensibly to forestall a German offensive in the area. Meanwhile, under Cheka direction, the two Latvians arranged a meeting between Lockhart and Colonel Eduard Petrovich Berzin, who commanded the Latvian Special Light Artillery detachment that guarded the Kremlin. Berzin had already been recruited and briefed by the Cheka. We don't know whether Berzin was a committed Bolshevik or whether his cooperation with the Cheka was opportunistic. Most likely the Cheka had promised him emoluments, such as support for eventual Latvian independence or hard cash. Berzin told the British diplomat that he was through with Bolshevism and that the Latvian units near Arkhangelsk could be induced to turn coat. The talk at this point seems to have been confined to Allied-Latvian cooperation against the Germans, not about overthrowing the Bolshevik regime.

But by mid-August the focus of the plotters' discussions had changed to the overthrow of the government. The Lettish regiments in Moscow and Petrograd were seen by Reilly and the other plotters as the key potential actors. Toward the end of the world war, hundreds of thousands of Latvians, including Latvian army regiments, had moved eastward into Russian territory to escape the German occupation of their homeland. They were welcomed by the Bolsheviks, who took allies where they could find them as civil war unfolded across Russia. The Soviets charged the Lett regiments—regulars, and certainly more trustworthy than the remains of the tsarist army—with guarding the Kremlin and the country's gold and munitions stocks, both in Petrograd and in Moscow. According to Hill, during those months the Lettish regiments were "the corner stone and foundation of the Soviet Government."

On August 15, Berzin and Buikis met in Moscow with Lockhart, Fernand Grenard, the French consul-general, and "Mr. Constantine" (Reilly). Lockhart and Grenard pledged Allied support for an independent Latvia, at the time under German occupation. Berzin said the Latvians would need financial assistance and promised that his troops would play ball. It was Grenard, apparently, who raised the idea of an anti-Bolshevik coup d'état—or, as one historian, Gordon Brook-Shepherd, put it, "the French Consul brought up the question of overthrowing the Soviet government and tied it in with the fate of Latvia." The Allied diplomats agreed to provide Berzin with funds. Lockhart, Grenard, and the American consul-general, DeWitt C. Poole, agreed to delegate Reilly to pursue the negotiations with the Latvians. Reilly was then given a "first installment" of 700,000 rubles—500,000 by the French and 200,000 by the Americans—to pass on to Berzin, and a few days later Lockhart gave Reilly another 700,000 rubles, from British coffers, to deliver.

After the plot's failure and Lockhart's arrest, Lockhart pretended that he had opposed the idea of trying to overthrow the Bolshevik government. He wrote that Reilly had asked him for his "opinion" on "the best use to be made of the Letts . . . [re] the possibility of a [counterrevolutionary] movement in Moscow." Lockhart had replied, so he said: "I saw no point in a movement in Moscow as . . . [there] was no one except the Germans to replace the Bolsheviks." All that he, the Americans, and the French had agreed to—as he put it in his report, "Secret and Confidential Memorandum on the Alleged 'Allied Conspiracy' in Russia," attached to his letter to Foreign Secretary Balfour on November 5, 1918—was "Reilly's plan to persuade the Lettish regiments on the front to cross over to our side," and when Reilly spoke of the need for "a movement" in Moscow, "we all demurred and pointed out that there was nothing to gain by this." Indeed, in his memoirs from 1932, Lockhart wrote that the three diplomats had "warned" Reilly "to have nothing to do with so dangerous and doubtful a [counterrevolutionary] move." The moneys given, he claimed, were for Berzin to organize Lettish cooperation with the British at Arkhangelsk.

Lockhart's version is buttressed by a statement by American Consul-General Poole to the British ambassador in Norway, Sir Mansfeldt Findlay. At the end of September Findlay reported that Poole, in Oslo on his way back to Washington DC, had told him that "an agent named Reilly . . . had . . . compromised Lockhart, who employed him in propaganda among [the] Letts, by exceeding his instructions and endeavoring to provoke a revolt against the Bolsheviks, or has even betrayed him. Reilly advocated encouraging a revolt, but Lockhart, after consulting [Poole] and the French Consul General, refused to do so." In this take, there was no "Lockhart Plot"—a figment of the Chekist imagination—only a Reilly Plot.

Lockhart, in his own summary of the affair, maintained that "I had no definite knowledge of the counter-revolutionary activities of the Allies in Petrograd." Of course, this was misleading, as the focus of the plotting was Moscow, not Petrograd. But Lockhart's statement was also an outright lie—as he unwittingly conceded later, in his report to Balfour. There he explicitly wrote that Cromie and MI6's Commander Ernest Boyce, both based in Petrograd, had worked with him and had passed on "considerable sums of [British] money" to the counterrevolutionaries. Lockhart was thereafter always to write of "Reilly's plan," but the evidence indicates that the plan was a joint Reilly-Lockhart enterprise and, indeed, from the first, a joint concoction of the Allied diplomats in Moscow, to some degree steered or advised by Reilly. (With Reilly, always forceful and always manipulative, it was never quite clear whether he was steering or merely advising the diplomats.) Indeed, Lockhart himself, from the spring of 1918, had been in close personal contact with anti-Bolshevik revolutionaries—all of them thinking and talking to him about counterrevolution and some actually busy preparing one—and had supported them financially. Most importantly, he met repeatedly with Savinkov's personal emissaries; indeed, in June Lockhart had even secretly met with Savinkov himself (in Moscow's Hotel Elite, Savinkov arriving in a French military uniform, with dark-tinted glasses). What remains in question is whether London—the Foreign Office and the prime minister—were aware of Lockhart's involvement in plotting the downfall of the Bolshevik regime. To be sure, from July Lockhart believed that he was carrying out London's wishes even though these were never made explicit to him; and to be sure, both Lockhart and London knew—or at least strongly suspected—that the Soviets were effectively tapping their communications, so that both London and Lockhart, in their exchanges, were very guarded and inexplicit in what they wrote.

Savinkov at the time headed the so-called counterrevolutionary Union for the Defense of the Fatherland and Freedom (also known as the League of the Regeneration of Russia). In his 1932 memoirs, Lockhart was abrasively dismissive of Savinkov. "I was not surprised," he wrote, that Savinkov in 1924 turned coat and "offered his services to the Bolsheviks." Savinkov, he wrote, was no "man of action." He was "a schemer—a man who could sit up all night drinking brandy and discussing what he was going to do the next day. And, when the morrow came, he left the action to others. . . . He had mingled so much with spies and agents-provocateurs that, like the hero in his own novel, he hardly knew whether he was deceiving himself or those whom he meant to deceive." He was also indolent. But, Lockhart conceded, Savinkov was "a forcible speaker," had written "several excellent novels," and "understood the revolution-ary temperament."

Nonetheless, Lockhart's communications with London during May and June clearly show that he was aware of the counterrevolutionary plotting and in continuous contact with the plotters. In May 1918, one of Savinkov's agents told Lockhart—according to a Lockhart report to London at the time—that "Savinkov's plans for counter-revolution" were based "entirely" on "Allied [military] intervention." He further noted: "Savinkov proposes to murder all Bolshevik leaders on night of Allies landing" and to establish a "military dictatorship." Indeed, according to Savinkov, the French already in March were pressing him to launch his coup, well before the prospective Allied intervention. Lockhart at this time also held meetings with members of another counterrevolutionary group, the so-called Center, led by Professor Peter Struve, Michael Feodoroff, and M. Avinoff. The Center was connected to the Volunteer Army and General Alexeyev. Moreover, the Foreign Office explicitly approved these "informal" contacts by Lockhart with Savinkov.

Reilly himself was later to write that Lockhart was "completely ignorant of my conspiracy, but the Bolsheviks were determined to drag the Allied missions into it." But this, surely, was written in order to help Lockhart, after his return to London, to rebuff his critics in the British establishment. Lockhart's son, Robin Bruce Lockhart, who wrote the first biography of Sidney Reilly (*Reilly: Ace of Spies*, 1967), later corrected this flagrant distortion. His father, he wrote, in fact "gave his active support to the counter-revolutionary movements with which . . . Reilly was actively working. . . . My father has himself made it clear to me that he worked much more closely with Reilly than he had publicly indicated."

MI6, for its part, later made an effort to square the circle. In its response to the Foreign Office, via Lieutenant Colonel C. N. French of the War Office (he was the WO liaison to MI6),

MI6 explained that Reilly had been sent to Russia as a "military agent" but that this function was "impaired" by Lockhart, who had used him for "some political purpose." What was that "purpose"? "Apparently" Lockhart "instructed" him to carry out "[political] propaganda." What exactly MI6 meant by that was left unclear—but the service was certainly alleging that it was Lockhart who had put Reilly up to going beyond his original, limited, "military" brief.

Back to the plot itself. On August 17, Reilly met Berzin at the Tramble coffee shop in Tsvetnoy Boulevard and handed him the initial 700,000 rubles, promising more. Reilly outlined the plan for "a counter-revolution in Moscow." The Latvian troops in Moscow, according to Reilly (as later related by Berzin to his Cheka handlers), were to "arrest all those present at the session of the Central Executive Council [meeting] including Trotsky and Lenin; to imprison them, to seize the State Bank, and central telephone Exchange and Telegraph. Then we [i.e., the Latvian commanders] were to announce to the people that order should be maintained in the city and everyone should abstain from politics until the arrival of the British military authorities." Reilly also had arranged for sabotage of bridges and rail links to Moscow and Petrograd in order to create food shortages, leading to chaos and popular resentment against the Bolshevik regime. As well, White Russian sympathizers in Moscow and Petrograd were expected to rise and join the Lett-led counterrevolution.

Reilly and Berzin met again two days later, when Reilly quizzed him on military matters. Reilly said "he'd provide a woman who would act as liaison between us." At their next meeting, on August 21, Berzin asked Reilly for more money. Reilly, for his part, informed Berzin that the Russian Orthodox patriarch Tikhon had promised to "conduct a service in the churches on the day following the coup in which he would explain to the people that the long-awaited for [*sic*] peace had come and no one needed to be afraid any longer. . . . After all this, he [Reilly] asked if I [Berzin] thought it'd be better to have Lenin and Trotsky shot on the day of the coup to avoid a situation in which Lenin might try and win the guards over to his side. . . . I answered . . . that I'd think the matter over." The following day Reilly handed Berzin another 200,000 rubles. (Western diplomats in Russia at this time had at hand stacks of rubles, mostly funds deposited with them by wealthy Russians for safekeeping. In exchange, the Russian depositors were given British government promissory notes, cashable in London at some future date.) Apparently Reilly and Berzin met again, briefly, on August 27, and again, but for the last time, in Petrograd, on the 30th. Both, incidentally, were to die, separately, at the hands of Soviet executioners a few years later.

Despite the Soviet clampdown on the ex-tsarist cadres following the Left SR rebellion in July, to Reilly it seemed that the conspiracy was well on the way to success: there were his as yet undiscovered networks in Petrograd and Moscow; the start of Western military interventions and subsidies; White military advances toward Moscow; and perhaps above all, the Latvian regiments, the Bolsheviks' praetorian guard, about to betray their masters and take over the Kremlin.

And then things fell apart. To be precise, on August 25 an assortment of French and American diplomats and secret service chiefs (it is unclear whether Lockhart also attended) met at the US consulate, with Grenard presiding. Reilly was also there, as was René Marchand, a French journalist working for *Le Figaro* whom Grenard had included under the mistaken belief that he was a French secret service officer. In fact, Marchand was an almost open Communist sympathizer and, less overtly, a Cheka informant.

According to Marchand, Reilly gave the attendees crucial details about the impending coup scheduled for three days hence: "On 28 August, a session of the All-Russian Congress of Soviets was to take place at the Bolshoi Theater, with the whole Russian leadership in attendance." Reilly and his co-conspirators would infiltrate the gathering and "at a signal given by Reilly, the Lettish soldiers would close all exits and cover the audience with their rifles, while Reilly, at the head of his band, would leap on to the stage and seize Lenin, Trotsky and the other leaders. All of them would be shot on the spot." (Later Reilly was to suggest that he had wanted them to be paraded around town "with their nether garments missing," rather than to be shot.) According to Hill, "it was decided [at the August 25 meeting] that the [the coup preparations] be handled by Lt. Riley." Marchand immediately passed on this information to Dzerzhinsky. A day or two later, Reilly and the others apparently decided to postpone the coup to September 6, when the Council of People's Commissars was due to meet with the Moscow soviet at the Bolshoi Theater.

The plot unfolded against the backdrop of Allied military interventions and Bolshevik clampdowns on internal enemies, real and imagined. The news of the Anglo-French landing in Arkhangelsk and the Japanese occupation of Vladivostok, along with rumors of the Czech Legion pushing toward Kazan, unnerved the leaders in Moscow. They were especially fearful of the Western powers. Weeks were to pass before they understood that the Allied deployment in Arkhangelsk was minuscule, a threat to no one. But in the interim, they "lost their heads." The Bolshevik leaders even started burning archives in Moscow and Petrograd. Lockhart, after a few initial days of elation, estimated that only "1,200" men had disembarked at Arkhangelsk (actually, the number was more than ten times as many—but still far from adequate to assault the Bolshevik power centers). Lockhart later charged: "To have intervened with hopelessly inadequate forces was an example of spineless half-measures which . . . amounted to a crime."

But in the initial days of uncertainty about the dimensions

and intentions of the Western intervention, the Bolsheviks worried about the threat of internal counterrevolution, despite the debacle weeks earlier of the Left SR uprising. The Bolsheviks launched a massive, almost indiscriminate, clampdown. On August 5 they even raided the French and British diplomatic missions in Moscow and arrested Lockhart's naval aide, Captain Alfred Hill, and other British and French officers, as well as European businessmen, visitors, and clergymen. In Petrograd, Cromie escaped a Cheka raid on the safe house he was staying in by jumping out of a window and hoofing it over a series of rooftops. After this, Cromie moved permanently into the embassy building (where his Russian mistress, Sonia Gagarin, had already taken up residence).

In Moscow, the Chekists narrowly missed both Reilly, who was not home, and the MI6's money hoard, which had been moved in time to the US consulate. At the British consulate, as the Chekists were arresting the local staff, British intelligence officers, on the floor above, were hastily burning documents and ciphers. The smell reached the lower floors—but the Chekists failed to catch on. "The Cheka was terrifying but far from clever," Lockhart concluded. Thereafter, Lockhart and other Western diplomats, while ostensibly free, were not allowed to leave for Murmansk or Arkhangelsk. In effect, they were hostages.

As for Russians, the Bolsheviks ordered all former officers belonging to tsarist veterans associations to report for new IDs and to undergo questioning. The move effectively broke the back of a potential White insurrection. Many anti-Bolsheviks were disarmed and/or arrested or confined to barracks outside Moscow and Petrograd. "In Moscow," reported George Hill, "the shattered remnants of these organizations came to me requesting that their men might be sent to Archangel, but owing to the shortage of funds, and the small likelihood . . . that they would be able to get through to the North, I informed [them] that it was impossible to help them."

Lockhart, for his part, anticipating the Cheka crackdown, had already in June "destroyed all" his "papers and documents" so that he could not be linked to any plots. The following month he pleaded with London to intervene lest the golden opportunity be missed.

It is possible that Lockhart was thinking of the Allied landing in terms of preempting a possible German takeover of Arkhangelsk or Murmansk rather than as a prelude to an Allied attack on the Bolsheviks in coordination with an anti-Bolshevik uprising by homegrown counterrevolutionaries. But the Bolsheviks viewed the Allied landings in the first week of August, in Lockhart's words, as "an outrage against international law"— and the Germans believed that the Allies intended to march on Moscow to depose the Bolsheviks (which is why their new ambassador, Karl Helfferich, immediately boarded a train for Berlin). According to Reilly, much of the Russian public, in Petrograd and Moscow, eagerly awaited an Allied military convergence on the new capital.

Following the early-August Bolshevik raids and arrests, Reilly and Hill went to ground and burned their papers. Hill instructed his assistant to "pay all the people who had been working for us, [and] to sell what was possible of our stores." Reilly found work—and presumably papers to go with it—in "a [Soviet government?] technical department," and Hill posed "as a film actor" with "an interest in a curio and fancy goods store." The two, using go-betweens, mostly Reilly's women, met occasionally in public gardens. They continued to collect intelligence about the Soviet military, especially about units and routes between Moscow and Arkhangelsk, to aid the expected Allied advance from the Arctic coast to the capital, and to oversee the "sabotage" work of their "destruction gangs," which were ready to damage the rail line along which the Bolshevik Saratov Division was expected to move northward, to counter the prospective British advance southward. (Earlier, since April,

French agents had been busy conducting sabotage operations, including blowing up aircraft, ammunition dumps, and bridges, to slow an expected German advance in western Russia.) In a subsequent report, Hill named two Russian officers, Lieutenant Colonel Mertzaloff and Captain Tchurieff, as the organizers of the sabotage gangs. By "22 August," Hill reported, he had "an extremely fine batch of men" ready to carry out the work of destruction; all in the past had suffered greatly at Bolshevik hands and had an axe to grind. Hill later received Britain's Distinguished Service Order (DSO) for blowing up the bridges between Vologda and Arkhangelsk. By the end of August the gangs had derailed Bolshevik ammunition and equipment trains, causing "three or four days' blockage."

According to Lockhart, following the Cheka crackdown in Moscow and Petrograd in early August the Soviet press had accused him of personally organizing "a plot for seizing the Soviet leaders, shooting Lenin and Trotsky, appointing a dictator, and taking command of Moscow." However, the Cheka refrained from arresting him, though presumably they kept him under surveillance. The destruction of the bridges leading to Moscow was also mentioned in the press, and was said to be aimed at causing starvation and triggering popular rebellion. Lockhart flatly denied everything. "Of such a plot I knew absolutely nothing. . . . I knew nothing of the proposed coup d'état." The Soviet press, according to Lockhart, named Reilly as "my agent [who] acted under my orders."

With Reilly and Hill playing possum, matters simmered for three weeks—and then all hell broke loose, just days before the planned coup was to be unleashed. On the morning of August 30, a military cadet, probably SR-connected, assassinated Moisei Uritsky, head of the Cheka in Petrograd. A few hours later—and far more significantly—Fanny ("Dora") Kaplan, a Socialist Revolutionary, shot and severely wounded Lenin as he was exiting a Moscow factory. (Lenin survived, but just barely;

his wounds may have contributed to the stroke that killed him six years later.) The Bolshevik press screamed revenge: "We will make our hearts cruel, hard and immovable so that no mercy will enter them. . . . We will kill our enemies in scores of hundreds; let them drown themselves in their own blood. Let there be floods of blood of the bourgeois—more blood, as much as possible." Karl Radek, the deputy foreign affairs commissar, declared: "For every head of ours, we shall cut off a hundred stupid bourgeois heads." The Cheka promptly unleashed what historians were to call "the Red Terror," beside which the clampdown of early August looked like child's play. Starting on August 30, over a fortnight, the Cheka rounded up and murdered some nine thousand real and imagined conspirators. The dead included twelve of Hill's courier network on the Moscow-Arkhangelsk route.

In Petrograd on August 31, Chekists raided the British embassy building and arrested most of the staff, including Boyce, the nominal head of MI6 operations in Russia (though the Chekists apparently didn't know this), and killed Captain Cromie, who had confronted them on the embassy's grand staircase shouting, "Clear out, you swine"; he then shot one or two raiders before himself being cut down in a fusillade of gunfire. According to British eyewitnesses, he was shot in the head and bled profusely. One of the Chekists reportedly kicked the supine captain as an embassy secretary tried to tend to his injuries. The Chekists pushed her aside and Cromie expired.

Reilly, who continued to evade capture, later told people that he had been in Petrograd that day and had been due to meet Cromie. When Cromie didn't show up at the designated café, Reilly had headed for the embassy. But as he approached, shots rang out. Brandishing his Cheka ID, Reilly asked what was happening. A soldier told him, and Reilly about-turned and headed back to Moscow.

Simultaneously, Cheka raids also hit British targets around

Moscow, including Lockhart's flat. Lockhart himself was briefly arrested and questioned about "Konstantin"'s (Reilly's) whereabouts. "The frightened face of Lockhart . . . I still recall as if it had been yesterday," Peters, the Cheka deputy head, later wrote. "He thought he was being charged with the assassination of Vladimir Ilyich [Lenin]."

On September 1, the Chekists arrested Elizaveta Otten, described by the Bolsheviks as "Reilly's chief girl," and Olga Starzheskaya, another of his mistresses. Both played dumb. But just as the Chekists were leaving their apartment, another Reilly agent, government clerk Maria Friede, oblivious, turned up. That proved the most significant of the day's arrests. She quickly fell apart under questioning. The Chekists then arrested her brother, Colonel Alexander Friede, an officer on the Red Army General Staff, who for months had passed key defense documents to Reilly (and to Xenophon Dmitrievich de Blumenthal Kalamatiano, who headed the American espionage network in the capital). On September 3, Dzerzhinsky and Zinoviev published an article in *Izvestia* stating: "The Anglo-French capitalists, through hired killers, have organized a range of terrorist attempts on representatives of the workers' government. Our native cities are crawling with Anglo-French spies. Sacks of Anglo-French gold are being used for bribing various scoundrels."

Most of Reilly's network, however, managed to evade capture, and the organization remained relatively "intact," according to Hill. Not so the Americans' network. Kalamatiano, an American of Greco-Russian origin who headed the American consulate's so-called Information Service, was away in Siberia, but he was picked up when he returned to Moscow later that month—carrying a hollowed-out walking stick containing documents about Red Army troop movements. Kalamatiano had no diplomatic accreditation and was to spend the next three years in a Soviet prison before being repatriated. Like the dozens of other British, American, and French officers and diplomats arrested in September, Kalamatiano was jailed with Russian criminals, "fifty to sixty in a room; their only sustenance was a daily helping of cabbage water and a little piece of black bread." (Kalamatiano, after release and repatriation, died in the United States in 1923, either from gangrene or metallic poisoning.)

Reilly, meanwhile, shuttled inconspicuously between his various women and undetected safe houses. But the Cheka arrested Lockhart and took him straight to the Lubyanka, the Cheka's HQ and prison. Lockhart kept a diary. "Very wet and beastly," he jotted down on September 1. But within hours, he was moved to more comfortable quarters, a spacious room inside the Kremlin walls, with an armed guard outside his door. He was gently interrogated by Peters, Dzerzhinsky's deputy, and Lev Karakhan, the deputy commissar for foreign affairs. Straight up he was asked two questions: Did he know "the Kaplan woman"? and "Where is Reilly?" According to Lockhart, the Cheka seemed to believe that he, Lockhart, was behind both the attempted assassination of Lenin and the wider Lettish plot. In an effort to eke out an admission of complicity, Peters at one point ushered Kaplan into Lockhart's room. Lockhart recalled: "She was dressed in black. Her hair was black, and her eyes, set in a fixed stare, had great black rings under them. Her face was colourless. Her features, strongly Jewish, were unattractive. . . . Doubtless the Bolsheviks hoped that she would give some sign of recognition." (There was none.) "She went to the window and, leaning her chin upon her hand, looked out into the daylight. And there she remained, motionless, speechless, apparently resigned to her fate, before the sentries took her away." Lockhart had never met Kaplan before and, at that point, knew nothing of the assassination attempt. She was executed the next day.

Lockhart was interrogated over the next few days, released, then re-arrested. The Soviet authorities apparently seriously considered executing him. Meanwhile, the Russian press ran "the most fantastic accounts of an Allied conspiracy which I [Lockhart] am said to be at the head [of] . . . the head and evil genius of everything!" Also briefly arrested was Moura Budberg (Marie Zakrevskaia), Lockhart's beautiful Russian mistress, the aristocratic wife of a tsarist diplomat (he was assassinated the following year). She was released almost immediately, apparently after agreeing to work for the Cheka (or after agreeing to sleep with Peters, or both). In the following days, she brought Lockhart "food galore and dainties of all sorts," as Lockhart wrote in his diary. Later, she was even allowed to stay with him for hours. Apart from Moura's offerings, Lockhart subsisted on "pea soup and potatoes—the same as the commissars get."

Lockhart used his time as a prisoner in the Kremlin well. Moura brought him books by Ranke, Thucydides, Renan, Carlyle, and Lenin. ("I was a serious young man in those days," he later wrote.) Into the Carlyle—*The French Revolution: A History*—Moura had slipped a piece of paper: "Say nothing—all will be well." Lockhart was released after four weeks, contrary to the betting among his guards, which was two-to-one that he would be shot, as most other Cheka "guests" were, routinely. Moura was to describe Lockhart, to his face, as "a little clever, but not clever enough; a little strong, but not strong enough; and a little weak, but not weak enough." But Moura was the love of Lockhart's life, as Lockhart, apparently, was hers.

Lockhart was released on October 2, after a month in custody, in exchange for the release of Maxim Litvinov, the Soviet representative in London, whom the British had taken hostage on hearing of Lockhart's arrest. Moura saw him off at Moscow's Nikolayevsky train station and waited until "the train [carrying Lockhart and, incidentally, George Hill] faded out of sight into the darkness." Lockhart reached London via Stockholm on October 19.

A few weeks later, both Reilly and Lockhart were sentenced to death in absentia by a revolutionary tribunal, the sentence to be carried out should either be caught on Russian soil. Other defendants were not as lucky. Reilly's mistresses told their Cheka interrogators that he had duped them. Olga said that she had "deeply loved" him and "intended to share my life with [him]." "I believed him and loved him, regarding him as an honest, noble, interesting and exclusively clever man, and in the deep [*sic*] of my heart I was very proud of his love." Elizaveta said that Reilly had been "foully deceiving me for his own political purposes, taking advantage of my exclusively good attitude to him." Both claimed they knew nothing of his anti-Bolshevik activities (which, most likely, was nonsense). Olga received a three-month prison sentence. Maria Friede received five years hard labor; her brother, Alexander Friede, was executed.

Moura, Lockhart's mistress, was not allowed to leave Russia with her lover. She subsequently wrote to him: "I love you, Baby, past all balancing or cool reasoning. I love you more than all the world . . . I lie awake repeating your name . . . my Baby." But she went on to have an interesting life, becoming writer Maxim Gorky's common-law wife. In 1929, the Soviets allowed her to move—or sent her—to London, where she served clandestinely as an "agent of influence" and collector of gossip for Soviet intelligence. But the British never arrested or tried her. She became writer H. G. Wells's mistress and moved in influential circles. She ran a literary-political salon, where people like Guy Burgess, Duff Cooper, Brendan Behan, Alexander Korda, George Weidenfeld, Anthony Blunt, Lord Bob Boothby, and Harold Nicolson were frequent attendees. For a living—apart from any money she may have received from the KGB—she wrote and translated books, including Gorky's works. She may also have spied on her friends and acquaintances, on and off, for MI5.

As to Lockhart, after a stint in the British embassy in Prague in 1919, he became a banker and, at the end of the 1920s, transformed himself into a journalist. For years, he wrote and edited a column in the popular *Evening Standard*, "Londoner's Diary." During World War Two, the government again needed his services, and he was appointed head of the newly created Political Warfare Executive, with the rank of undersecretary of state, orchestrating British propaganda to Axis-occupied Europe. Occasionally he and Moura would spend evenings together. He died in 1970, after publishing more than a dozen books, mainly on international affairs. Moura died four years later.

In his November 1918 memorandum to Balfour, Lockhart firmly denied that Reilly was a Bolshevik agent-provocateur— as DeWitt C. Poole, the US consul-general in Moscow, appeared to believe. (George Hill, in *his* report after returning to Britain, averred that "I consider that Lt. Reilly has been most unjustifiably libeled.")

Indeed, over time Lockhart's opinion of Reilly grew more and more positive, though he tried to retain a modicum of balance. In his memoirs, published in 1932 after Reilly's death, he wrote that Reilly was "a man of great energy and personal charm, very attractive to women and very ambitious. I had not a very high opinion of his intelligence. His knowledge covered many subjects, from politics to art, but it was superficial. On the other hand, his courage and indifference to danger were superb." Lockhart wrote that "he was a Jew with, I imagine, no British blood in his veins. . . . [But] I never questioned Reilly's loyalty to the Allies." Lastly, Lockhart wrote, Reilly "was a man cast in the Napoleonic mould." What he apparently meant was reflected in Colonel Norman Thwaites's assessment in his autobiography, *Velvet and Vinegar*, also published in 1932. Thwaites wrote: "Behind all Reilly's efforts lay the conviction that some day he was destined to bring Russia out of the slough and chaos of Communism. He believed that he would do for Russia what Napoleon did for France."

But the plot had failed; indeed, the planned coup never really got off the ground. It was preempted and nipped in the bud by the massive Chekist crackdowns of August–September 1918. Reilly, Hill, and their co-conspirators lay low through the Red Terror, which, within weeks, was to claim thousands of lives. Reilly apparently spent some of the time rooming with a whore dying from syphilis in a Moscow brothel. "It is very often just these fallen women who are greater patriots than their more respectable sisters," Reilly later wrote. "I did not spend two nights in the same place or under the same name," he recalled. "Now I was a Greek merchant . . . now I was a Tsarist officer, seeking escape from Moscow, now I was a Russian merchant, trying to avoid the military service." When night fell, Reilly would "creep around to one of the addresses. . . . The door would be poked slightly ajar and a quavering, frightened voice would ask who was there. The formula was always the same. 'Serge Ivanitch' . . . told me you would allow me to sleep here tonight. . . . Rarely, I fear, I was a welcome guest. My coming would reduce my hosts—or hostess-to-be—to a pitch of the most extreme terror. . . . I would see their lips twitch and their eyes go blank with nameless terror, and their whole bodies would quiver and shake as if in an ague, but I was never refused." Reilly successfully evaded the furious Chekist dragnet. For a few days, when they lost touch, Hill feared Reilly had been taken—but then was reassured by one of Reilly's girls. The two spies eventually met up and Hill gave Reilly his own identity papers, in the name of George Bergmann, a Baltic German art dealer. At the end of September, Reilly entrained to Petrograd, somehow finagling his way into a compartment reserved by the German embassy. He spent the ride discussing politics and art with "fellow" Germans. From Petrograd he sailed to Reval (Tallinn), then under German occupation, and after a few days mixing with German officers boarded a boat to Helsinki. He reached London on November 8.

The captain of the tugboat that conveyed Reilly to Helsinki, Harry van den Bosch, a Dutch engineer, later described the experience. His story tells us something about Reilly. Van den Bosch related that one night a young girl came to see him in Reval and asked if he could take on board someone who was "in trouble." He agreed. A few hours later Reilly showed up and said that he was a German antiques dealer. When they reached Helsinki, Reilly disembarked, van den Bosch none the wiser. But Reilly had left the captain a sealed package containing a letter, in German, dated October 10. It was a telling admixture of truth and lies. It read:

> My dear van den Bosch, I feel that after everything you've done for me, I must not leave here clothed in all the lies I had to use, and that I owe it to you to say who I really am. I am neither a "Bergmann" . . . nor an art dealer. I am an English officer, Lt. Sidney Reilly, RFC. . . . [I] have been for about six months on a special mission in Russia, and have been accused by the Bolsheviks of being the military organizer of a great plot in Moscow. . . . The Bolsheviks have done me a great honour . . . and they have put a great price on my poor head. I can boast of being "the most sought after man" in Russia. . . . I am not an art dealer but an art collector, and can even boast of being among the experts. My Napoleonic collection is really among the biggest in the world. I have really studied in Heidelberg and am a D. Phil. . . . I have been engaged for many years on state matters in Russia: for part of the war I was a purchasing agent of the Russian Government in Japan and America. . . . I am married, and cannot refrain from saying, to a woman [Nadine] whom I consider to be the most charming, the prettiest and the bravest woman in the world. My wife lives in New York, and the poor thing has heard nothing from me these last months. . . . So I believe I have confessed everything. . . . It is very possible that I shall be busy at the peace conference in resolving the Russian question. Then we shall meet in the Hague. . . . Probably I shall return to Russia, but from the other [White] side, and I hope that then, for a change, the Bolsheviks will run away.

(It is worth noting that Reilly at this point apparently knew, or guessed, that his MI6 bosses had in store for him an expedition to southern Russia and attendance at the Paris Peace Conference, which wrapped up World War One.)

The Russian press reports that September about the "Lockhart plot"— mentioning Reilly by name—were picked up in newspapers in the West, triggering an effort by Reilly's first wife, Margaret, then living in Belgium, to locate her husband. Presumably she wanted money. She contacted the British Interests section in the Netherlands legation in Brussels (which was still under German occupation) but got no response. The following month, she wrote directly to the War Office in London: "Since the outbreak of war I am absolutely without a word or message of any kind from him." Subsequently, the British minister in Brussels informed her that Reilly had been in Russia and had escaped to Finland. "I desire ardently to hear from [my dear husband]," she wrote. "My financial situation is also rather strained." Apparently, Margaret's letters—which were passed on to MI6—prompted Hill to ask Reilly about her. Reilly responded: "I have no wife. There is nothing to discuss." Reilly persuaded C to order Hill to stop looking into the matter—but Reilly sent her £10,000, and she returned to Brussels. According to Hill, to stop her interminable "nagging," Reilly had also threatened to kill her.

5

Southern Russia

ONE OF THE best-documented and, intelligence-wise, most productive chapters of Reilly's life was his sojourn in southern Russia, along the Black Sea coast, during December 1918–March 1919. No sooner had he returned to London from the failed Moscow coup attempt than he was asking C to be sent back in. C initially was hesitant. No doubt the failure of the Reilly-Lockhart plot, which he probably had not directly authorized, coupled with the occasional allegation that Reilly was actually working for the Bolsheviks, played a part. And in the background, as always, were Reilly's origins and dubious business reputation. The Foreign Office, officially and in private conversations, objected to Reilly's continued employment by His Majesty's Government.

Reilly spent November 1918 in London energetically lobbying his friends and contacts to put in a good word. He bombarded Lockhart with letters. In one, he wrote that although he was "keen" on returning to his "wife and . . . business, I consider that there is a very earnest obligation upon me to continue to serve. . . . I feel that I have no right to go back to the making of dollars until I have discharged my obligations. I also venture to think that the State should *not* lose my services. . . . [If] a halfway decent job would be offered to me, I would chuck business altogether and devote the rest of my wicked life to this kind of work." Reilly even said that he would be willing to serve "under" Lockhart (whatever that meant—Lockhart himself had just returned from Russia and was awaiting a new posting). Lockhart appealed to C, and within days C spoke to the Foreign Office. C decided to send Reilly back to Russia, but this time under Foreign Office economic "cover" and with access to FO facilities in Russia.

Reilly clearly owed Lockhart a debt. But he also understood the nuances of Lockhart's attitude toward Bolshevism. Before departing for Russia, Reilly wrote to his former co-conspirator: "In-so-far as this [Bolshevik] system contains practical and constructive ideas for the establishment of a higher social justice, it is bound by a process of evolution to conquer the world, as Christianity and the ideas of the French Revolution have done before it, and . . . nothing—least of all violent reactionary forces—can stay its ever-rising tide." Reilly went on to praise the institution of the "soviets," the workers and soldiers councils, as "the nearest approach, I know of, to a *real* democracy based upon true social justice and . . . they may be destined to lead the world to the highest ideal of statesmanship—Internationalism."

But all of this was in the nature of a caveat. The thrust of Reilly's letters to Lockhart at this time was altogether different. The problem with Bolshevism, he wrote, was that it had "run amuck," and was liable to spread to Germany, indeed, "over the entire world." The current Bolshevik ideal of a Dictatorship of the Proletariat had as its avowed objective "the extermination or complete strangling of all non-proletarian classes" and would

result in "the destruction of all attainments of cultural, eco-
nomical and political chaos [*sic*; order?] and extinction of all
liberties and of all principles of justice." This, in Reilly's eyes,
was "a far greater danger" than "Prussian Militarism"; in his
eyes, the world was unsafe until "the firebrands of destruction
are wrested from the hands of the Russian Bolshevists." As he
summarized, "The salvation of Russia has become a most sacred duty which we owe not only to the untold thousands of
Russian men and women who have sacrificed their lives because
they trusted in our promise of support, but also to ourselves for
there can be no permanent peace in the world nor any security
for civilization whilst two hundred million people occupying
one-seventh of the earth's surface are seething in inextricable
chaos and rapidly reverting to savagery. Believe me, my dear
Lockhart."

On November 30, the Foreign Office agreed to Reilly's
dispatch, with an "assistant"—George Hill—to southern Russia.
The FO mandarins doubtless regarded the level-headed Hill as
a potential curb on Reilly's expected enthusiasm. C and Reilly
met on December 3, for the first time since Reilly's return from
Petrograd. Reilly described his activities in Russia. How C re-
acted we don't know, though he could not have been unimpressed by the story of Reilly's months-long successful evasion
of the Cheka and escape to England. On December 12, C summoned Hill and Reilly together. He explained that "certain
important information about the Black Sea coast and South
Russia was wanted for the Peace Conference" that was due to
assemble in Paris at the end of the year. So off they went—after
C had submitted Reilly's name for a Military Cross for his previous escapades in Russia.

The situation in southern Russia in December 1918, as in
the country as a whole, was infinitely complicated. The White
forces had rebounded from the initial defeats of winter 1917/
1918, when local Bolshevik urban militias aided by forces sent

by train from Petrograd and Moscow (in the so-called railroad war) overpowered local Socialist Revolutionary Party and pro-tsarist "rebellions." During spring–summer 1918 White armies rebounded, taking control of much of the south, in the area bounded to the north by Orel and Liski (next to Voronezh) and in the east by Tsaritsyn and Piatigorsk, encompassing the Don and Kuban regions and some of southern Ukraine. From November to December 1918, following the defeat of the Central Powers, most of Ukraine was loosely (though only for a few months) held by local Ukrainian nationalist forces, with the southeastern corner occupied by White Russians or foreign troops (French, British, and Greek).

The White forces, consisting of the Don Cossack and the Kuban Cossack hosts, and the Volunteer Army (VA) under General Anton Ivanovich Denikin (following the deaths of Generals Alexeyev and Kornilov) held parts of southern Ukraine and adjoining areas encompassing Rostov (abandoned by the German army in November 1918), the Sea of Azov, Ekaterinodar (the VA's headquarters), Novorossiysk, the Crimean Peninsula, and Odessa. Denikin's forces, more than forty thousand strong, consisted of former tsarist army officers, Kuban Cossacks, and locally recruited peasants. Denikin was both commander-in-chief of the VA and the political-administrative ruler—actually dictator—in the area.

The White Russian forces were indirectly backed by contingents of Western troops, who moved about the Black Sea and some of its ports. An Anglo-French naval squadron arrived in Novorossiysk at the end of November 1918 bringing French and British military missions to Denikin's HQ at Ekaterinodar. In December, a French force 1,800-strong, composed mostly of Senegalese troops, landed in Odessa, and was soon joined by Czech, Greek, and Polish units. While public opinion in Britain and France remained staunchly opposed to involvement in new wars, their governments felt free to supply, within limits, the White armies with food, equipment and money, and some token backup units.

That was the scene when Reilly and Hill reached Odessa. For Reilly it must have been a moving moment and experience, the return to his former stamping ground—and not as a penniless youth but as an agent of an imperial power, his adopted country. It had taken Reilly and Hill a fortnight to get there. They had left London on December 12, 1918, and reached Paris the following day. The train ride was not uneventful. They had shared a compartment with Ignacy Jan Paderewski, the famous Polish musician, who was on his way to Paris to head the Polish delegation at the peace conference. (The following month he was elected Poland's prime minister.) Paderewski had apparently been a close friend of Reilly's mother during Reilly's childhood, and the two talked over old times. According to Hill, the meeting between the two men "showed that Reilly knew Paderewski very well and that Paderewski knew Reilly's half sister [Anna]."

Late on the 13th, Reilly and Hill pressed on to Marseille, a "nightmare trip . . . packed like sardines in a first-class carriage" together with "scores of badly wounded French soldiers" making their way home, as Hill recalled. A Greek warship then conveyed the two spies, along with the newly appointed British consul-general in Odessa, John Picton Bagge, to Malta, where they switched to a British cruiser bound for Constantinople. They lunched on board HMS *Lord Nelson* with Admiral Somerset Gough-Calthorpe, commander of the Mediterranean fleet, and then boarded a minesweeper to Sevastopol, where they disembarked on December 24.

The two spies posed as "English merchants keen on reopening trade between England and the Black Sea ports." Reilly telegraphed his first report ("Despatch No. 1") to London, via the consulate in Odessa, four days later, after meetings with senior White Russian officers and officials, including General

Lukomsky, Denikin's minister of war, and Admiral Kanin, his minister of marine. Reilly told them that he was working for the British government and interested in more than commercial opportunities. Reilly reported directly to SIS and the Foreign Office, but not to the director of military intelligence, which annoyed the War Office, as Hill later recalled ("the DDMI [deputy director of military intelligence], a Colonel Kish [i.e., Frederick Hermann Kisch, later chairman of the Palestine Zionist Executive, 1923–1931], . . . as a Jew was very sore at not [*sic*] being kept in the dark").

In that first report Reilly described the political, economic, and military situation along the northern shore of the Black Sea and advised on the requisite British policy. There was "general economic chaos" (no local manufacturing) and political disunity, with several different governments operating in the region. The "only concrete dependable" military force, Reilly reported, was Denikin's Volunteer Army, with a total strength of "150,000" and a field force of "60,000" (both figures were exaggerations). But the VA's future depended "entirely" on the Allies' attitude and material aid, wrote Reilly, for it was acutely short of weaponry, clothing, and munitions. Denikin, he reported, got on well with the local authorities in Crimea. But there were "numerous" Bolsheviks lying low on the peninsula, awaiting an opportune moment to rebel. And Odessa along with much of the coastline was governed by the French (as had been agreed between Britain and France the year before in "Terms of the Convention Agreed at Paris Dated 23rd December 1917," which defined the English Zone as consisting of "the Cossack territories, Caucasian Armenia, Georgia, [and] Kurdistan" and the French Zone as consisting of "Bessarabia, Ukraine, Crimea"). Reilly recommended that Britain enable the Volunteer Army to "occupy [the] entire Black Sea littoral." As to the area to the north, Reilly dismissed as ephemeral the Ukrainian national rising led by Symon Petliura against the Bolsheviks after the German army's departure. It would be overwhelmed by the Bolsheviks unless the Allies intervened militarily, he accurately predicted.

As the weeks passed, Reilly, who sent London twenty reports in all from southern Russia, became increasingly advocative. In his second report, of January 8, 1919, after meeting with most of Denikin's aides, he described the VA as the "pivot" of the situation, an army controlling "a considerable portion of Sothern and South-Eastern Russia." He praised "the exalted patriotism and the statesman-like sagacity of its late leader," General Alexeyev, and described Denikin as loyally carrying out his legacy. He praised Denikin's "absolute honesty . . . political moderation, immense popularity and . . . [unwavering] loyalty to the Allied cause," as well as his intention to distribute land to the peasantry. Denikin's main problem was unifying, under his command, the dispersed White armies, Kolchak's in the east and Krasnov's Don Cossacks to the immediate north.

Reilly argued that Denikin did not require or ask for Allied troops to fight his battles, but he did need some to garrison conquered towns and guard his lines of communication. In a (slight or major) deviation from this line, however, he supported Captain Hill's proposal that the Allies provide Denikin's columns with air support "to throw the Bolshevik troops into panic. The effect of bombing, contour chasing and machine gun strafing would be of the greatest value," Reilly wrote. The Kazan-born Hill, an airman by training, opined that "a great number of R.A.F. men would gladly volunteer for this service." Reilly also called on the UK to send a "High Commissioner with wide powers" to the region. Perhaps he had himself in mind. The economic situation in the region was chaotic, and Reilly recommended that the Allies immediately print 500 million rubles of tsarist money for Denikin's use. In return for such aid, Denikin would give the Allies "long term concessions for timberlands, mines, cotton-growing territory, waterpower, railways, etc." He warned that the Red Army was growing by leaps and bounds under Trotsky's command and was the only well-fed body in Bolshevik Russia.

The newly arrived British consul-general in Odessa, Picton Bagge (who during 1928–1937 was to serve as director of the Foreign Division in Britain's Department of Overseas Trade), thought the Reilly report "most able and concise . . . and . . . deserving of close study." Bagge supported Reilly's call for greater British investment in a White victory. Bagge, Reilly, and Hill all took an instant dislike to General Poole, who headed the British military mission to Denikin. Bagge lamented Poole's "weakness for female society," while Reilly, more specifically, lambasted "Madame P.," Poole's mistress, as "an [exceptionally] ugly woman."

Ironically, Reilly at the time was busy pursuing a local Russian lady, "K," while trying to ward off fresh appeals by his wife Margaret, whom he had abandoned more than a decade earlier in Port Arthur. In January 1919 she had written to several British government departments requesting money. As one War Office official, Colonel Pennington, commented, "These wives of Reilly are somewhat tiresome." (He was referring both to Margaret and to Nadine's request at this time for help to travel to or stay in the United States.) A few weeks later, having been informed of Nadine's letter, Reilly asked MI6 to "please pay Mrs. Reilly [i.e., Nadine] for [*sic;* from] my account 100 sterling. Please inform her I shall [make?] further provision after I return." As for Margaret, from that point on Reilly periodically paid her "hush-money," according to Hill.

Bagge noted that the British military mission officers in the area reciprocated Reilly's negative view of them, as reflected in his attitude toward Poole. "Certain British officers did not care for him, perhaps out of jealousy, for Reilly is certainly exceptionally able, and gets on extremely well with the Russians," wrote Bagge—the implication being that the British officers did not. All the senior Russian generals in Ekaterinodar regarded Reilly as "*persona gratissima*," wrote Bagge, quoting Hill. The British officers no doubt found this annoying. But Bagge's worst barbs were directed at the French officers in the area. They "have managed to alienate the sympathy of all parties and classes" in Ukraine and Crimea, and were "the most tactless of people." Not only that, but "the French seem to have no idea how to handle the Russians . . . and easily get angry." Odessa's inhabitants blamed the French for the lack of food in the town—because they had failed to clear away the brigand bands that controlled the town's access roads and were barring food supplies. Bagge was completely taken with Reilly—and taken in completely by the persona Reilly projected, of an Irish-born British officer (despite Reilly's accent, which was neither Irish nor English). Moreover, Bagge seems not to have suspected that Reilly was a Jew.

Bagge's view of the French occasionally slid into anti-Semitic gossip, which he passed on to London. Among Odessans, he wrote, only "the Jews" had "close and friendly" relations with the French, "exasperating the Russians, the more so as the Jews are, and always were, Germanophile." General d'Anselm, the commander of the French forces in the area, "was to be seen at the theatre arm in arm with a Jew lawyer who had been expelled from the Society of Lawyers. French officers were continually in the society of rich Jews, and go about with Jewesses. The so-called Consul, Henno, is the *comble* [Fr: the limit]. His mistress, a Madame Bernstein, whom her husband refuses to divorce, he introduces as his wife, and had the effrontery to bring her as such to a public dinner, at which she was put in the place of honour, and I was next to her. She is present at all interviews he gives, and takes part in them. I believe though this was too much for even d'Anselm, and that Henno leaves in a few days for Paris."

Reilly seemed to at least in part attribute the promiscuous

French behavior to Bolshevik machinations. The Bolsheviks were using "money, women and all forms of entertainment" to undermine French morale, he reported. But using the same means, they made little headway with the British troops, he added.

Reilly and Hill spent much of their time touring the Volunteer Army's area of control, meeting with generals and officials. But they never, it seems, visited the (very nebulous) front lines. The bulk of their time was spent in the region's cosmopolitan city, Odessa, which suffered from material shortages, political upheaval, and general uncertainty about the future. The two spies, however, seem to have enjoyed themselves, though the town's culinary offerings left something to be desired. Hill later described a meal he took with Reilly and Bagge: "Our dinner consisted of caviar, which was not fresh, beefsteak, coffee with some cream in it, four mandarins and one bottle of ordinary red wine." Reilly told Bagge nothing about his youthful connection to the town. At one point, however, when Hill and Reilly strolled past a certain house, Reilly "turned pale," Hill later recorded—or as Hill told Robin Lockhart, R. H. Bruce Lockhart's son and Reilly's first biographer, decades later, Reilly had "a hysterical fainting fit."

Reilly and Hill at last met Denikin on January 10, 1919. Hill described him as "a short, sturdy Slav, with a pointed grey beard and a close-shaven head." Reilly was only marginally impressed. Denikin, he wrote, was "broad-minded, high-thinking, determined and well-balanced," but he lacked "great power of intellect" and "those characteristics which mark a ruler of men."

Although his focus during those months was on the south and the Volunteer Army, Reilly nonetheless continued to press upon his superiors in London his old recipe for the overthrow of Bolshevism in the Soviet heartland. That January, Reilly reported "strong unrest" among the Lettish troops in Moscow, who "constitute the greatest latent danger for the Bolsheviks." "Like nearly all mercenaries throughout the ages they will desert their masters in the hour of danger," he predicted. He recommended embarking on an anti-Bolshevik propaganda campaign in Latvia, promising "autonomy" and a blanket pardon for Lettish troops who may have committed crimes while serving the Bolsheviks or Germans.

No doubt Reilly read newspapers from and about the Soviet zone, met travelers and anti-Bolshevik couriers from Moscow and Petrograd, and may himself, during those months sojourning in the south, have traveled north in one guise or another. His descriptions of conditions in the Soviet core area sound first-hand and accurate, if tendentious. In his "Despatch No. 8," from the end of January, he described the Bolshevik-governed area as a territory completely isolated from the rest of the world and inhabited by a populace unaware of what was going on outside Russia. The food situation was "terrible," with only "cabbage and potatoes" available to the mass of the people. Although the army was well fed, among the civilians, meat, flour, sugar, and fish were available only to industrial workers, and these were strictly rationed. "The greater part of the population is in a continuous state of hunger. . . . Horses which fall in the street are immediately pounced upon and cut into pieces by ravenous people, [this] is a frequent spectacle," Reilly reported. Russia's towns and villages were ravaged by typhus and other diseases. "The poorer people are buried in sacks in mass graves." Fuel was virtually unavailable. All factories had been nationalized, but industry was at a "standstill" as raw material stocks were almost depleted. "The Red Terror continues unabated," with peasant risings multiplying and villages being flattened with artillery and subjected to atrocities. Much of the intelligentsia was working for the Soviets out of "hunger." According to anti-Bolshevik sources, whom he quoted at length, the bulk of the population "impatiently awaits" liberation by the Allies and the White armies.

But Reilly was also critical of the Volunteer Army, for its

often ineffective administration, unpersuasive propaganda, the prevalence of the black market in its area of control, and the corruption rife in its junior officer corps, where commissions were bought and sold. Pepita Bobadilla, Reilly's last wife, was later to write that Reilly regarded the White Russian officials and officers as largely "vain, talkative and ineffective." But he also criticized Allied behavior toward the Whites—for example, their utter failure to help the Whites set up a navy of their own in the Black Sea.

Like Bagge, Reilly was particularly harsh in his criticism of the French. Two months after the French takeover of the Odessa region, Reilly berated the "deep estrangement between [the] French Command and [the] Volunteer Army." While Denikin and his aides promoted the notion of a large united Russia, the French generals actively worked to partition the former tsarist domain into several statelets. One of those envisioned by the French was a "federation" consisting of Ukraine, Poland, Belarus, and the Don basin. The French were busy hammering out an agreement with Petliura, the Ukrainian separatist. Reilly believed that the French command's aims were supported locally by "mostly Jewish" elements of the population—which were "pro-German," he argued. He feared that such a federation would itself be pro-German.

Reilly reported that "the absence of the British is universally regretted [in Odessa]." The "charitable" view, he wrote, was that French behavior was due to deficient officers, not to policy dictated from Paris. Reilly's complaints, reinforced by Bagge's reports, left their mark in London, which in January–February 1919 made "representations" to Paris, perhaps on the basis of the assumption that the French officials in Odessa were not adhering to government policy.

Side by side with his continuous appeals for immediate Allied economic aid, Reilly—looking to the *longue durée*—pleaded for Allied help in the economic regeneration of White Russia

through a restructuring of the country's economy, to be facilitated by a British-American takeover of the Russian banking
system. He wrote of Karol Jaroszyński, a Polish financier and
sugar magnate, as the possible fulcrum of such a regeneration.
He persuaded Bagge to ask the Foreign Office to allow Jaroszyński to come to London to cut a deal with British financiers;
and in May 1919, after Reilly had returned briefly to New York,
he urged Bagge to promote a Jaroszyński visit to the US, where
bankers and capital could be mustered to further the scheme.
Reilly and Bagge formulated a master plan for a British (or Anglo-
American) syndicate or banking combine that would buy out or
buy into the Russian banking system, and from there orches-
trate the vaunted Russian economic recovery. No doubt Reilly,
the perennial middleman and fixer, also saw the scheme as an
avenue to personal enrichment.

Reilly's focus was on the grain trade and mining, mineral
and timber concessions, and transport companies, in all of which
Russian banks figured prominently. Bagge put it succinctly in a
memo to the Foreign Office: "Great Britain should secure control of the big banks in Russia [through a London-based "Central Bank," with Jaroszyński as one of its directors], of the big
transport companies, and of the insurance companies." Winston Churchill, whom Reilly roped in (according to Hill, they
were introduced in March or April 1919 during the Paris Peace
Conference), was perhaps the most enthusiastic supporter of
the Whites in the British cabinet, and also viewed economic assistance to Denikin as the key to White survival or victory. As a
Jaroszyński aide wrote in a paper circulated by Churchill, then
British secretary of state for war and air, "If England will not
give this assistance, Kolchak and Denikin will perish." Churchill
himself wrote Foreign Secretary Curzon on October 19, 1919,
that "the Bolsheviks are failing . . . [and] their regime is doomed,"
and he quoted Bagge in his letter: "They may pass like a heap of
snow melts under a hot sun, leaving behind only the dirt which

it had gathered." Churchill concluded that Britain must now help the Whites by "fostering a union of Russian and British financial interests, such as is now projected, in order to establish good conditions of credit and trade in the enormous areas newly liberated from Bolshevik rule by Denikin."

But Lord Curzon and the Foreign Office mandarins were wary, seeing the scheme as reactionary and directed toward restoring tsarism. Indeed, commenting on Churchill's letter, one FO official, perhaps the permanent undersecretary, Lord Hardinge of Penshurst (the signature is unclear), wrote: "[Regarding Churchill's] reference . . . to the Yaroshinski scheme: On brief acquaintance he does certainly not inspire confidence. His scheme is fantastically colossal and should be approached with infinite caution. The man is an honest genius, multi-millionaire or bankrupt (he himself does not know which)." A few weeks earlier another FO official had expressed displeasure at Jaroszyń-ski being under the control of "somebody called Reilly, a dangerous character who had been in the German Secret Service [*sic*]."

Before this exchange of letters and minutes, the Jaroszyń-ski scheme briefly appeared to make headway. In July 1919, leading Russian bankers signed an agreement with Jaroszyński naming him "president" of a "bankers' council." In August, the scheme was presented to the British Treasury. Sir John Bradbury, the Treasury's permanent undersecretary, was hesitant, however. "We ought to see the colour of his money first," he wrote—meaning that Jaroszyński should first produce a handful of bona fide Anglo-American bankers committed to the scheme. Curzon was more upbeat: "While I am unable to express my opinion as to the financial and commercial merits of Mr. Yaroshinski's proposals . . . I am told that one of his main objects is to provide this country with the means, through the control of banking institutions in Russia, to prevent Germany from reasserting the predominant position in the field of Russian finance and commerce." If the British Treasury authorities showed themselves to be "satisfied that the scheme is financially sound . . . I may say without hesitation that we shall be prepared to give the group such support as lies in our power."

But Treasury approval was delayed, nervous American and British bankers refused to commit, and in October, as Churchill was pressing the scheme on his cabinet colleagues, Denikin's advance on Moscow collapsed, as did Kolchak's in the east. Meanwhile, the White commander in Russia's northwest, Nikolai Yudenich—though supported by British aircraft dropping chemical weapons (the "M Device") on the Red Army—failed to reach Petrograd. And the Reilly-Bagge-Jaroszyński plan finally collapsed.

Throughout Reilly's stay in southern Russia, Consul-General Bagge was enthusiastic about his abilities, schemes, and reports. In February 1919 he recommended that Reilly "proceed home" to report in person to his superiors—or alternatively, proceed directly to Princes Island, off Istanbul, the venue of a planned conference between Allied and Soviet officials. Reilly agreed. He, too, saw his work in southern Russia as "completed"; staying on would be "a waste of time," time better spent elucidating the situation in person to British policy makers back home.

Reilly's other main proposal, echoing Denikin's wishes, that large British forces help bolster the Whites by garrisoning newly occupied towns and securing supply lines, seems to have gained some traction in London. Given Allied "exhaustion" and Russia's size, "[an Allied] invasion and occupation of Russia at the present time is not considered to be a practical military proposition," wrote Sir Henry Wilson, the chief of the Imperial General Staff, in February 1919. The Allies should focus on ensuring the integrity of the breakaways—Finland, Estonia, Latvia, Lithuania, Poland, and Romania—whose national aspirations they generally supported. Moreover, Arkhangelsk and Murmansk should be evacuated as soon as weather permitted. But Britain should go forward with supplying Kolchak with stores and advisors, and Denikin with weaponry ("tanks, aeroplanes, armored cars, guns, machineguns") and instructors ("all volunteers"), as well as "holding [with 'two divisions'] the country south of the Caucasus and the Black Sea and Caspian Sea" to secure Denikin's "rear and flanks" (what Wilson meant by that "south of" description is unclear). Wilson urged the Allied governments to "issue a definite statement of policy" along these lines. The present uncertainty about Allied policy only raised Bolshevik morale and reinforced Bolshevik propaganda, and undercut those of the White forces. We don't know whether Wilson actually saw Reilly's dispatches or recommendations in the raw; but his recommendations, to the extent that they are intelligible, seem to have been influenced by the Reilly dispatches.

Some, if not all, of Reilly's first twelve dispatches reached London via Bagge's consular telegraph lines. But on March 1, 1919, all his past typewritten reports were brought to Whitehall in person by Captain Hill on his return to Britain. We know that Foreign Office officials (and probably MI6 executives) took them very seriously. One official, Reginald (Rex) Leeper of the FO's Political Intelligence Department (and later, the founder of the British Council), minuted that they "have always been very interesting and reliable and there is no one else in S. Russia who can give us the political information we require." Walford Selby, of the FO's Russia Department, remarked: "These dispatches contain a fund of useful information . . . [but] I do not know that there is any particular action which we can take." Upgrading economic aid to Denikin and appointing an Allied high commissioner to southern Russia depended on a political decision by all the Allies to generally upgrade their relations with the Whites. Selby recommended sending the Reilly dispatches to the British Peace Delegation in Paris and to the Department of Overseas Trade. Another official, "S.G.," referring to Reilly's call for launching anti-Bolshevik propaganda, said that work along those lines was already being done with the press, including "sending consignments of illustrated English newspapers for distribution in S. Russia." (Who exactly in southern Russia would read such newspapers is unclear.) In addition, literature in Latvian had been distributed "in the North." Leeper said that Reilly's mooted return to London would be a "great loss" and recommended that Reilly should remain in southern Russia, his position regularized. Perhaps he could be appointed "secretary" to a high commissioner, should one be appointed, Leeper suggested.

In the end, Reilly's reporting from southern Russia had little effect on policy or history. Indeed, as Christopher Andrew, a leading historian of British intelligence, concluded more generally, the reports by all SIS agents in Russia during those years "had no significant influence on British policy to[ward] Bolshevik Russia."

In early March 1919, a few days before Reilly's departure for England, the military-political situation in southern Russia reached a "critical" point, the persistent dissonance between the British and French turning into a clear rupture. In Bagge's estimation, which was also Reilly's, French tactlessness, even "rude[ness]," had alienated the Volunteer Army, as had their separate bilateral negotiations with the Ukrainian separatist leadership, the so-called Direktoriat. Should France and the Direktoriat reach an agreement, signaling French support for the breakup of Russia and, perhaps, acquiescence in Bolshevik rule in the Russian heartland, it would be akin to "agreement with a corpse," wrote Bagge. His argument was that the Ukrainian separatists had no real power base or army. He also opposed British recognition of Georgian independence. The dismemberment of Russia only played into German hands, thought both Bagge and Reilly.

But the French and the Direktoriat concluded a draft agreement around March 7, 1919, with the French recognizing the "Democratic Republic of Ukraine." One of its key clauses barred the Volunteer Army from operating in Ukraine. According to Reilly, the agreement and French policy played "into the hands of Bolsheviks and Germans and must result in disaster." On March 7, Reilly reported on the dissolution of Ukraine's armed forces and their "catastrophic disorganization." The different bands, no more than large gangs, were pillaging the countryside "and produc[ing] [anti-]Jewish pogroms." This was one of the few references in Reilly's accessible reports to the dire situation of the Jews in civil war Russia, where tens of thousands were slaughtered and raped by White (and at times, Red) troops. Occasionally, Reilly reported generally about "atrocities"—as in his cable of February 18, 1919 ("Despatch No. 13"), referring to Bessarabia—but without identifying the victims. At other times, he conveyed what amounted to derogatory comments about Jews without adding his own assessment, as when, on March 6, in his last dispatch to London before leaving Odessa, he wrote that Denikin considered "all Jewish officers . . . undesirable for active service" in his Volunteer Army.

(Recent research credits Ukrainian nationalist forces, especially Petliura's followers, with responsibility for 65 percent of civil war–era anti-Jewish pogroms, while 17 percent were carried out by Whites, especially Denikin's troops, and some 8.5 percent by the Red Army's First Cavalry Regiment/Corps under Semyon Budyonny.)

The British officials in Odessa, with whom Reilly was in constant touch, were well aware of the massive anti-Jewish pogroms taking place in areas of Ukraine to the north—in "Gitomir[,] Berditsche[,] Ourutsch[,] Ostrog[,] Elisavettrad[,] Balta[,] and Proskouroff and . . . dozens of neighbouring towns and places," as Oscar Grousenberg, a local lawyer and politician, put it in a cable to the Board of Jewish Deputies in London, transmitted by the British consulate in Odessa on February 28, 1919. In June 1919, Captain George Hill, Reilly's colleague, wrote in a lengthy, comprehensive report on what he had seen and done in southern Russia that "the Jewish question has become one of the most burning questions throughout Russia. Not only is the press, platform [politicians?], and public opinion engaged in the discussion, but pogroms have already broken out. Anti-Semitic feeling is so strong that a large Jewish pogrom throughout the country seems inevitable. The seriousness of this cannot be gauged yet, but it is certain that their duration greatly depends on the opposition [to pogroms] Bolshevism puts up. The longer and more bitter the struggle against the Soviets, the more sanguinary the pogroms." Hill seemed to imply that White Russians equated Bolshevism with the Jews and, hence, attacked Jews.

Of course, far more obtrusive in the minds of British officials in Odessa during early 1919 was the "French problem." Bagge appealed to London to intercede in Paris to block the signing of the Franco-Ukrainian agreement. Admiral Richard Webb, the acting British high commissioner in Turkey, regarded French infidelity as so "grave" that he summoned Reilly to Istanbul to tell him about it "in person." Paris, of course, denied supporting Ukrainian separatism and blamed Denikin for the VA-Ukrainian-French rift, for failing to halt the Bolshevik advance southward, and for undermining French operations in the Ukraine.

Throughout, the British feared imminent French collapse—and they were right. By early March 1919, most of Ukraine was in Bolshevik hands. On March 10, the Red Army marched into Kherson as Bolshevik sympathizers rebelled inside the town—"men and women firing from roofs and windows." According to French reports, "the French and Greek [occupation forces] fought admirably," but were overwhelmed. The French claimed that their troops had suffered 40 percent casualties. Nearby Nikolayev fell to the Bolsheviks a few days later.

Nonetheless, in mid-March Bagge still felt that there was "no military danger to Odessa." The Red Army units in the area were small, there were very few Bolsheviks inside the town, and two Greek divisions, one and a half French divisions, and assorted Polish and VA troops were deployed in the area. It was vital that Odessa—"the financial, commercial, and shipping centre of South Russia"—be held, Bagge opined. But the French, he said, were "scared and contemplate evacuation." Bagge pressed London to immediately appoint an "officer of high rank" as a liaison in Odessa, with Reilly as his "secretary." In addition, the Volunteer Army's presence in the area should be expanded, he suggested.

In the weeks before the final collapse, the French seemingly tried to sort out the mess, establishing in Odessa a "Council of Defence" that was charged with handling the food distribution problem, naming the revolutionary turned businessman Pinhas Rutenberg to head the effort. Reilly and Bagge supported the proposed measures as well as Rutenberg's appointment, but it was all too little, too late.

Bagge (and Reilly) did not know it, but Paris and London had already secretly decided to abandon Odessa. At a meeting in Paris on March 25, 1919, between the Allied "Big Four"— Lloyd George, Wilson, Clemenceau, and Orlando—the British prime minister asked whether, given the limited amount of supplies and transportation available, precedence should be given to Romania or Odessa. General William Thwaites, the director of military intelligence, representing the British army, said that although holding Odessa was important for morale, it was of "greater importance to supply the needs of Roumania." The French army's commander, Marshal Ferdinand Foch, concurred. So the Big Four agreed "at once [to] divert to Roumania" equipment originally earmarked for Denikin, Foch arguing that supplying Denikin—who, he said, headed an army "which had no Government behind it"—was as good as throwing equipment into the trash can. Lloyd George was "pleased . . . very much" by Foch's assessment, stated the report on the meeting. "It was decided to evacuate Odessa, only this is very 'hush,'" Thwaites recorded.

Bagge and Reilly had failed to convince London of Odessa's crucial importance. The town rapidly descended into chaos: food supplies no longer reached town, and people were murdered in the street for their overcoats, it was reported. On March 28, French forces, aided by Greek troops, swept through "the low Jewish quarters of the town" and arrested more than a thousand "suspects and vagabonds," also seizing rifles. On April 3, Bagge's deputy, Consul Henry Arthur Cooke, advised "all British subjects to leave." The French and Greek troops evacuated Crimea and then began to withdraw from Odessa, but not before throwing "a good deal of ammunition into the sea." Trotsky at this time told his British lover, the sculptor Clare Sheridan, that "France is just a noisy hysterical woman." On April 5, the French and Bolsheviks agreed on a peaceful handover, and the next day Bolshevik patrols "were to be seen everywhere in town" as Allied ships set out to sea. Cooke deemed the evacuation "uncalled for [and] . . . a colossal blunder"; Allied prestige had suffered "deplorably." The British charged that Germany was behind the Bolshevik campaign in southern Russia. In August, Denikin's forces were to briefly recapture Odessa, but the Bolsheviks reentered the town when the White armies collapsed in February 1920.

By then, of course, Reilly was long out of the picture. Indeed, he had left weeks before the collapse. Already on February 22, 1919, he had cabled London: "Have completed my work here [Odessa]. . . . May I respectfully suggest that I be ordered to return home as my further stay here is a waste of time." After some dithering by London, Reilly left Odessa for Istanbul around March 8. He reported there to Webb on March 10, and then journeyed to London, which he reached a week or so later.

But MI6 barely afforded him a breather, for he set off immediately with Hill for Paris. MI6 left the two spies' "status" and mission "vague." They were told simply to "hold [them] selves in readiness to give expert information" on southern Russia at the peace conference and, more generally, to "observe what was happening." Initially, they were lodged in the Hotel Majestic, the headquarters of the British delegation, but they soon moved to the Hotel Mercedes. Perhaps the rates were cheaper—or perhaps their superiors sought to distance them from the British delegation to assure clandestinity.

The city was crowded with dozens of national delegations and spies, with soldiers of the various Allied armies also passing through. "The restaurants were always full," Reilly recorded; "there were innumerable official receptions, dinner parties and balls, and endless private luncheon and supper parties. A continuous round of gaiety formed the background of the laboring peacemakers." He met with a wide range of people including, for the first time, Winston Churchill, who, like Reilly, was obsessed with Russia and the Bolshevik threat. Over drinks, Reilly—always very forward—buttonholed Eleutherios Venizelos, the Greek prime minister, who was also staying at the Mercedes. The two had apparently met before, perhaps in Salonika (Thessaloniki) in 1916. Venizelos told Reilly about Greece's territorial ambitions, prefiguring the Greek army's occupation of Smyrna (Izmir) in May 1919. Reilly also met up with Rutenberg, who had fled Odessa just before the Bolsheviks marched in. It is likely that the two discussed Zionism and Palestine, though we have no record of what was said.

But Reilly probably spent most of his time in Paris enjoying himself—in night clubs and cabarets, or gambling. His favorite haunts were La Rue Restaurant, on the corner of Rue Royale and Boulevard de la Madeleine, and Maxim's.

We know nothing about Reilly's input at the peace conference—whom he advised (except, perhaps, Churchill), what he told them, or what effect, if any, that advice may have had—except for one episode that left traces in the accessible documentation.

Reilly apparently had a hand in scotching Soviet participation in the peace conference. The Soviets, eager to acquire international legitimacy and recognition, dearly wanted to attend. But most of the participants regarded the Bolsheviks as pariahs, and they were not invited. Soon after Hill and Reilly settled into the Mercedes (March–April 1919), two American officials arrived in the city, secretly charged by President Wilson with engineering Soviet admission to the conference. One of them was William Bullitt, Wilson's sometime emissary to Moscow (later, the first US ambassador to Moscow, and co-author with Sigmund Freud of *Thomas Woodrow Wilson: A Psychological Study*). Hill and Reilly got wind of the Bullitt mission, apparently hearing about it from the Estonian American Sergius Riis, an intelligence officer who was a member of the American military delegation—and then shared their intelligence with two British diplomats, Walford Selby and Harold Nicolson. The two spies then leaked the story—perhaps after receiving the go-ahead from the two diplomats and presumably after receiving approval from MI6—to Henry Wickham Steed, a British journalist who wrote for the *Times* (London) and the *Daily Mail*. The two newspapers published the scoop—and the American démarche was dead in the water. (A few months later Wickham Steed, by then editor of the *Times*, endorsed the anti-Semitic forgery *The Protocols of the Elders of Zion* and, by the way, blamed "the Jews" for the outbreak of World War One.)

By mid-April, MI6 decided that there was nothing more Reilly could usefully do in Paris, and he and Hill went their separate ways. Reilly sailed for New York, hoping to meet American businessmen. It is likely that C was persuaded of the advantage to British interests of the Reilly-Bagge-Jaroszyński scheme, designed to bolster the fortunes of the White Russian cause. In the United States Reilly met with prominent bankers, including Samuel McRoberts. But nothing concrete emerged, and he returned to England the following month.

Hill, for his part, was sent back to southern Russia and was eventually (in December 1919) appointed intelligence officer to the newly installed British high commissioner to the region, the geographer and former director of the London School of Economics Halford John Mackinder. Ironically, Hill had more or less landed the position Bagge had sought for Reilly (and perhaps Reilly had sought for himself) earlier that year. The anti-Bolshevik Mackinder, who was at the post for only a few months, unsuccessfully tried to mobilize increased Allied support for the White Russians. But the Volunteer Army had steadily lost its appeal. Having occupied Odessa and southern Ukraine in August–September 1919, VA units, apparently without Denikin's authorization, unleashed a series of pogroms against the region's Jewish communities. And the battle against the Bolsheviks was going poorly. The VA registered one last brief success when, in October, it conquered Voronezh and Orel, some two hundred miles from Moscow. But after that, things went rapidly downhill. Denikin's army was overstretched, the tide turned, and the Red Army swept relentlessly southward as the winter snows thawed. In March 1920 the Reds took Ekaterinodar, the VA's HQ, and it was all but over. Denikin and his troops, humiliated, retreated to Novorossiysk and were evacuated by boat to Crimea. In April, Denikin quit his command and fled to Southampton. He was succeeded by General Pyotr Wrangel, but the remnants of the VA in Crimea proved unable to withstand the Red Army for long. In November 1920, following a slowly constricting siege, the VA survivors evacuated the peninsula. Wrangel lived out his remaining years in Turkey, Serbia, and Brussels, where he died—possibly poisoned by Soviet agents—in 1928. Denikin died in Ann Arbor, Michigan, in 1947.

6

Farewell to the SIS

According to Alexander Orlov, a senior NKVD (KGB) officer who in the 1930s had had access to the organization's files, Reilly during 1918 had provided London "with a regular supply of fairly accurate information about the Red Army, the doings of the Soviet government and the political happenings in Russia." Indeed, he had been a first-class gatherer of intelligence, at least until his networks in Moscow and Petrograd were rolled up by the Cheka, and had provided London with first-class intelligence from southern Russia afterward. But gradually, following his return to Britain in March 1919, a distance developed between Reilly and MI6. He remained on the payroll and continued to go on missions to the Continent, and he still produced useful intelligence—such as a long report, from September 1920, on clandestine Bolshevik operations, including a detailed list of Bolshevik agents in Western Europe. Hence, it is no surprise that in October 1919 the SIS petitioned the War Office to upgrade Reilly from RAF lieutenant to honorary major in the army, given his "important work for the Foreign Office." (That promotion never came through, apparently because of financial considerations, though a few months later Reilly was awarded the rank of captain.) But by the end of 1920, he was out (though Reilly's War Office file—"jacket 258152/1"—says he was "placed on [the] unemployed list" already on April 24, 1920).

The divorce between MI6 and Reilly was a gradual process. His final ejection from the organization was set in motion in the autumn of 1920, when C sent him to Poland—possibly his last official mission as an MI6 officer. By then, the Poles had won their brief war against the Ukrainian nationalists (November 1918–July 1920) and were about to end their war with the Soviets (February 1919–October 1920), wars fought over the borderlands between the new Polish state and its neighbors to the east. The Polish defeat of the Ukrainians, leading to the occupation of chunks of Ukrainian territory, triggered the war with the Soviets, who continued to regard Ukraine as part of their domain. After seesaw campaigns, the Poles eventually beat the Soviet armies, taking control of about half of Belarus (the new borders were formalized in the Polish-Russian Treaty of Riga in March 1921).

C sent Reilly to Warsaw to report on Polish-Ukrainian relations and on the Polish-Soviet war. Reilly at the time feared "an alliance between German militarists and Russian Bolsheviks mainly with the object of attacking Poland"—prefiguring the Nazi-Soviet pact and the German and Russian invasions of Poland in 1939. Reilly sent London a "list of 58 Bolsheviks" (that is, Bolshevik agents) working in Eastern Europe. In summer 1920, at Reilly's suggestion, Cumming began to set up a pan-European "anti-Bolshevik intelligence service [i.e., network]." Reilly, Paul Dukes, and Vladimir Gregorievich Orlov, a former tsarist Okhrana officer, toured Western and Eastern Europe and recruited anti-Bolshevik operatives (five in Warsaw, eleven in Riga, four in Reval, three in Helsinki, and fourteen in Berlin). Some were members of their country's intelligence services. In December 1920, Reilly reported to MI6 that "a tremendous amount of spadework [had been done] and that everything now depends upon how it will be utilized." Orlov was designated the network's coordinator or mastermind. But in the course of the following year nothing came of the work invested, and the network evaporated.

Meanwhile, to more lasting effect, Reilly reestablished contact with his old anti-Soviet colleague from Moscow, Boris Savinkov, who was now based in Warsaw. As Reilly wrote to Paul Dukes in October 1922, the current generation of Russian exiles were a write-off, a set of "has-beens." But Savinkov was something else. "Savinkoff was and is and always will be the only man outside of Russia worth talking to and worth supporting. . . . He has kept his organization both here and in Russia alive, and he is the only man amongst the Russian anti-Bolsheviks who is actually working. . . . I am sticking to him through thick and thin and . . . I shall continue to do so until I find a bigger man." (Reilly also supported funding the education of the children of exiled Russians throughout Europe, in the belief that eventually they would contribute to "the resuscitation of Russia.")

Savinkov was the central figure in the anti-Bolshevik plotting by Russian exiles in Europe. But the Foreign Office in London viewed Reilly's growing attachment to Savinkov with suspicion, given Britain's desire by late 1920 to end the state of belligerence with the new Russian regime. Savinkov was seen by the bulk of the British establishment, especially at the FO, as a fly in the ointment, a born troublemaker, a "terrorist" and a "nihilist"—"most unreliable and crooked," according to Eyre Crowe, the office's permanent undersecretary. Toward the end of 1920 Savinkov was launching anti-Soviet guerrilla raids into Soviet-held territory—in one of which Reilly, Crowe later claimed, participated.

But, of course, it was not just Reilly's connection with Savinkov that led to his dismissal from MI6. Anti-Semitism, rife in the British military and intelligence establishments, may also have played a part. Reilly, as all strongly suspected, was a Jew and very much looked the part—and besides, he had an ungentlemanly reputation for shady financial dealings.

But there were other, probably more important, factors at play. In the years immediately following the end of World War One, against the backdrop of general demobilization and painful budget cuts, the SIS allocation was severely reduced, and C was forced to let go dozens of agents and close down a string of foreign stations. Moreover, while Russia had become in 1917 a key focus of MI6 operations, and was to remain so during the following two postrevolutionary years, with the Bolsheviks busy subverting "bourgeois" regimes and the capitalist order in the West and with a civil war raging across Russia, by the end of 1920 the civil war was all but over, Britain had pulled its troops out of Russia, and official London was set on burying the hatchet. The need to spy on Russia had considerably diminished and there was little use for Reilly, whose cover had been blown and who was under an official Soviet death sentence.

The thaw in Anglo-Soviet relations was slow but steady. Already on January 16, 1920, the Allied Supreme Council had announced the end of the trade blockade of Soviet Russia, and a peaceful "exchange of goods" was posited. In May, the Soviet commissar for foreign trade, Leonid Krasin, arrived in Britain and embarked on open bilateral trade negotiations (albeit while other arms of the Bolshevik government, especially the Comintern, were still engaged in subversion and propaganda inside the United Kingdom). Churchill, refusing, in his words, to "shake hands with the hairy baboon," declined to attend the meeting with Krasin at 10 Downing Street. Curzon, for his part, reluctantly shook Krasin's hand after Lloyd George chided him with "Curzon, be a gentleman." A year later, the British signed a trade agreement with the Bolshevik government and, on February 2, 1924, shortly after Britain's first Labour Party–led government took office, accorded the Bolshevik regime recognition and formally established diplomatic relations. (Needless to say, between March 1921 and 1924 the Bolsheviks continuously violated the trade agreement, which had stipulated that the two sides halt mutual subversion and propaganda.)

But although Reilly had been let go by SIS, he was far from letting go of Bolshevik Russia. The overthrow of the Bolshevik regime, which he continued to regard as the bane of civilization, had become his personal obsession and mission, much as it was for Savinkov.

Savinkov was a colorful, sinister, multifaceted character, a revolutionary activist with the soul of a (fairly successful) novelist (*The Pale Horse*, 1909). He came from a middle-class Russian family in Kharkov, Ukraine, where his father served as a judge. As he matured, he became politicized. He studied law at St. Petersburg University, where he was arrested for anti-tsarist plotting and exiled to Vologda. In 1903, he fled to central Europe and joined the Socialist Revolutionary Party, quickly rising through the ranks in its "combat" wing. In 1906, he was sentenced to death for his part in the assassinations of Vychaslev von Plehve, the tsarist minister of the interior, and Grand Duke Sergei Alexandrovich, a major tsarist court figure. But Savinkov managed to escape from an Odessa prison and reach France, where he served in the French army in World War One. In 1917, hard on the heels of the February Revolution, he returned to Russia and served as deputy war minister in Kerensky's provisional government. After the October Revolution he went underground and founded the secret anti-Bolshevik Society for the Defense of the Motherland and Freedom. In 1918, after the failure of the Socialist Revolutionary uprising he had led in Yaroslavl, he returned to Paris, where he was Admiral Kolchak's representative. During the Polish-Russian War he moved to Warsaw and organized and launched anti-Bolshevik operations.

Reilly came to view Savinkov as the chief "hope of his country," though Reilly's future wife, Pepita Bobadilla, was unimpressed. After their first meeting in London in 1923, she thought him "a great disappointment"—but she kept her "unfavourable opinion" to herself. This is how she described Savinkov after that first meeting: "A portly little man [who] strutted in with the most amusing air of self-assurance and self-esteem—a little man with a high brow, a beetling forehead, little eyes, and an undershot chin. The little man posed in front of the mantelpiece. Now he gave up a view of one side of his profile, now of the other. Now he thrust his hand into his breast in the approved Napoleonic manner, now he flourished it in the air with a theatrical gesture. Every pose was carefully studied." Pepita was an actress, so she knew.

But others aside from Reilly took Savinkov seriously, Winston Churchill, as we have seen, among them. He described Savinkov as a man "without religion . . . without morals as men prescribe them, without home or country, without wife or child, or kith or kin [actually, Savinkov had a wife and child and other relatives], without friend, without fear, hunter and hunted, implacable, unconquerable, alone." Savinkov's life, Churchill concluded, was "devoted to a cause . . . the freedom of the Russian people."

Starting in late 1920, Reilly provided Savinkov, who was routinely broke, with funds, as did Brigadier Sir Edward Spears, the intelligence officer who had headed the British military mission in Paris in 1920. Spears subsequently went into business with Reilly. But, according to Spears, Reilly's total identification with Savinkov, the man and his mission, got in the way of their joint business ventures, which included importing radium, a chemical element believed at the time to have medical curative power, from Czechoslovakia. "R[eilly] has I fear compromised his position in Prague by identifying too much with Savinkov who is now out of favour there." Spears chided Reilly for "dealing with shady people and mixing politics with business." Both men probably hoped that Savinkov would open up business opportunities for them in Russia, come the counter-revolution.

Post–World War One, Reilly, too, was often short of cash. Although he sporadically made large sums in his various business ventures, he was a high-liver and gambler, and overly generous with his friends. In May 1921, strapped for cash, he auctioned in New York City much of his Napoleonica collection, consisting of "literary, artistic and historical properties illustrative of the life of Napoleon Bonaparte." According to the *New York Times,* Reilly made close to $100,000 at the auction (more than $1 million in current values). Savinkov seems to have gotten wind of the windfall, for the following month his aide, the writer Dmitry Filosofov, pressed Reilly for further contributions to his boss's war chest, arguing that the anti-Bolsheviks' hopes rested on money—"money, money, money."

In summer 1921, employing subterfuge, Reilly managed to obtain a visa for Savinkov to enter Britain, where he wanted to raise funds, recruit activists, and deliver lectures. Reilly also arranged meetings for him with key government figures. C was not amused by Reilly's antics. C's disaffection was encapsulated in a cable of February 1, 1922, from MI6 to Vienna station: "Give [Reilly] no more information than [is] absolutely necessary. . . . He [already] knows far too much about our organization. . . . He is [now] Boris Savinkov's right-hand man, and it is probably Reilly who is financing the whole [anti-Bolshevik] movement. . . . He is exceedingly clever, certainly not anti-British and is genuinely working against the Bolsheviks. . . . [But] be careful not to tell him anything of real importance. . . . The last thing in the world we should wish is to become embroiled in any way with

Savinkov." Reilly continued to believe that "the fall of the Bolshevik Government is inevitable, whether it is next year or in three years or in ten." Of course, Reilly was right—but he was off by some seven decades.

Savinkov, according to his mother, Sofya Alexandrovna Savinkova (née Yaroshenko), regarded Reilly as "a tower of moral strength," "a knight without fear or reproach" (so she wrote Reilly in December 1922). Clearly, Savinkova wasn't referring to Reilly's personal life. Most of his lovers were of the demimonde—actresses and showgirls—or else colleagues' wives. Among them was Eleanor Toye, a professional dancer and a sister-in-law of Edward Toye, a friend of Lockhart's. In the early 1920s she occasionally worked as Reilly's secretary. Some of her typing no doubt was connected to Reilly's latest business venture, buying and selling diamonds with a new business partner, none other than Leonid Krasin, the head of the Soviet economic mission in London.

It was at this time that Reilly conducted one of his more unusual affairs. Caryll Houselander stands out, if only because in later life she became one of Britain's leading Catholic mystics, the author of spiritual religious texts (*The Way of the Cross, The Reed of God,* etc.). Born in Bath and educated in a convent school, Houselander from a young age had visions, most of them featuring Jesus Christ. When she paired with the forty-five-year-old Reilly, she was an eighteen-year-old art student at the St. John's Wood Art School.

As she matured, Houselander developed a keen interest in Russia, which then was a deeply religious Christian land. The interest turned into an obsession. She later related that in 1918 she had had a vision auguring the assassination of Tsar Nicholas:

> I was on my way to buy potatoes [apparently off Finchley Road, London], hurrying because I had been warned that they were wanted for dinner. . . . Suddenly, I was held still, as if a magnet held my feet to a particular spot in the middle of

the road. In front of me, above me, literally wiping out not only the grey street and sky but the whole world, was something which I can only call a gigantic and living Russian icon. . . . It was an icon of Christ the King crucified. Stretched on a cross of fire in a vestment which blazed and flamed with jewels, crowned with a great crown of gold . . . His head bowed down by the crown, brooding over the world.

Shortly after, in the same street, Houselander saw posters announcing the tsar's assassination as well as his picture in a newspaper. It was the face she had seen in the vision, she realized. She came to believe that it would be through Russia that Christ "would return to the world and take possession of all mankind."

The enchantment with Russia led to her enchantment with the dark (Russian) stranger who was to be the (human) love of her life. He was not particularly handsome, "certainly not photogenic," according to Maisie Ward, Houselander's biographer. But he looked "haggard and tortured," and had "a high sloping forehead, smoldering eyes, and sensuous lips," Ward was told—"and in a man such looks may be more exciting than beauty."

Reilly, of course, was at least equally obsessed with Russia. And he also shared with Houselander an acute interest in Jesus Christ. Indeed, Reilly once said that he thought "he was [a resurrected] Jesus Christ." And the two shared an interest in art (though Reilly, perhaps, more in a commercial sense).

They met in 1920 when a friend of Houselander's, Della Foster, who had Russian émigré friends, showed Reilly (whom she later described as "very brusque") some of Houselander's sketches. Reilly was interested. Foster eventually brought the two together, and Reilly bought a few of the sketches. Perhaps he liked them, or perhaps he saw them as a way into Houselander's bed. In any case, Houselander was smitten. Or as she later put it, "I was . . . swept by temptation as dry grass is swept by a flame." "She was," Ward observed, "young and hungry for love." Reilly, for his part, may have seen something special in her. He was soon providing her with a small weekly allowance. This went on for two years. Decades later, now a fully fledged Catholic mystic, Houselander recalled: "A man who was a very great friend of mine and who was . . . at one time a spy . . . became a friend of Rasputin's." (We don't know whether this was true or just one of Reilly's inventions.)

Houselander continued to hold Reilly dear long after he was reported killed in Russia. He appears to have been her only lover. "The years have not lessened or dimmed the love [I felt for him]," she wrote a friend in the 1940s. According to Houselander's biographer, the affair ended precipitately when she heard that Reilly had fallen in love with Pepita Bobadilla, whom he married in 1923.

Pepita Bobadilla (a variant of her stage name, Josefina Bobadilla, which she had adopted in 1914) was an actress, and she often matched Reilly in inventiveness. She claimed to have been born in Ecuador (or, alternatively, in Argentina or Chile), but in fact, Nelly Louise Burton was born, on January 20, 1891, in Hamburg, Germany, the daughter of English-born Isobel Burton, a servant, and her lover, Franz Brueckmann, a German businessman. Nelly grew up in London. She began working as a dancer in 1910 and in 1912 moved to Paris, joining the risqué Moulin Rouge cabaret. After it burned down in 1915, she returned to London, where she was hired as a chorus girl by the impresario Charles B. Cochran, a successful stager of musicals. In 1920 she married the Australian-born dramatist Charles Haddon Chambers. He died five months later, leaving her a fairly wealthy widow. (Her story in some ways echoes that of Margaret Thomas, Reilly's first wife.)

She may have first met Reilly backstage, briefly, after one of her appearances in London in early 1922. But their first real meeting took place in December that year, in the coffee lounge of the posh Hotel Adlon in Berlin. A few days before, also at the hotel, she had heard his praises ("the most mysterious man in Europe") sung over tea with a British delegate to the Reparations Commission, then meeting in the German capital, and a German naval ex-officer. The German told her that he had met Reilly, whom he called "an ace of espionage," when Reilly was spying in Germany during World War One. He and his fellow officers were so impressed by Reilly's intrepidness that they had been happy to hear that he had made it safely back to Britain.

That evening, she got her first glimpse of Reilly, who had already "assumed heroic proportions in my imagination": "when raising my [blue] eyes from my coffee, I found them looking straight into a pair of brown ones at the other side of the room. . . . I felt a delicious thrill run through me." It was love at first sight. She found him "well-groomed and well-tailored," "with a lean, rather somber face, which conveyed an impression of unusual strength of resolution and character." She thought his eyes were "steady, kindly and rather sad"—but his expression was also that "of a man who not once but many times had laughed in the face of death."

Reilly, too, appears to have been enamored at first sight (Pepita was beautiful, and her relative wealth may also not have proven a hindrance). He immediately sought and engineered an introduction through the unnamed British delegate. Again his eyes sent a thrill through her. They talked about European politics, the Cheka, the war. By the end of the week they were engaged. They had swept each other off their feet.

After Pepita underwent an appendicitis operation and Reilly had made brief excursions to Prague and Paris, the couple were married on May 18, 1923, at the Register Office in Henrietta Street, Covent Garden, London. Reilly's MI6 buddies George Hill and Stephen Alley served as witnesses, alongside Pepita's sister, Alice Menzies.

During the following years, indeed until Reilly's death, Pepita noted his devotion to his adopted country, but also to "the rehabilitation of his beloved Russia." She became au courant with the "small groups of [Russian] exiles" "plotting, planning, conspiring" in Berlin, Paris, Prague, and London. Helsinki, she found, was "absolutely seething with the counter-revolution." She later recorded that Reilly was no monarchist. He sought not the restoration of the Romanovs, but rather Savinkov's installation as the "future dictator" of Russia.

7

Savinkov

By the early 1920s, his new love and marriage notwithstanding, Reilly cut a rather sad figure. He had been cut loose by the British establishment—MI6—and was going on broke.

Reilly spent most of his remaining years on earth trying to make money. He first paired up with retired Brigadier Spears. They traveled to Prague together in July 1921, where they set up a tobacco company. Spears later recalled Reilly's "great generosity" in tipping "the band playing in the restaurant in an island" in the middle of the city. Subsequently, they established the Radium Corporation Ltd., geared to selling Czech radium in Western Europe. They dined with Lockhart, now the commercial secretary in the British legation in Prague, and sought his help. But not much came of all this—and Spears eventually caught Reilly skimming expenses and failing to pay utility bills. They made little money, or none at all, and in mid-1922, at Spears's initiative, they parted company, though they remained on friendly terms. Spears always had a soft spot for the colorful, charming, and articulate spy.

Back in London, Reilly reverted to the pull of patent medicines. Once again he partnered with Weinstein, his confederate from New York, and a man called Hugh Coward to found Modern Medicine Ltd. They began to produce a "medicine" called Humagsolen, destined for the US market. But it, too, made little money, and in July 1923 Reilly sailed with Pepita to New York—their boat fares covered by a loan from an old SIS acquaintance, Major "Robbie" Field Robinson. He hoped to stimulate interest in Humagsolen as well as to pursue his legal claims, originally launched in US courts in 1920, against the Baldwin Locomotive Company, whose munitions sales to Russia during the war he claimed to have brokered.

Although Spears provided him with letters of introduction and recommendation, Reilly made no headway among Chicago's businessmen in garnering investments in Modern Medicine. (The company filed for bankruptcy in 1925.) Meanwhile, in 1924, the New York Supreme Court ruled against Reilly's claim for $542,825 from Baldwin Locomotive. He was so angry during the court proceedings, recalled Paul Dukes, who apparently attended a session, that he literally "foamed at the mouth. It was not a pretty sight."

In England again, Reilly remained keen on making money. He even reached out to Spears at the end of 1924, after setting up yet another company, Trading Ventures Ltd.: "Could not we do something together" in New York, he asked, perhaps promoting American, British, or British colonial bond sales to "foreign municipalities and foreign industries"? Also, export-import deals between the US and Britain, selling "British inventions," might be of interest, he suggested. But nothing came of any of this.

His efforts to make money were driven partly by his desire to finance Savinkov and the counterrevolutionary cause, also in perpetual financial crisis. Savinkov received donations from sympathizers and occasional contributions from the intelligence services of anti-Soviet governments. But as Soviet Russia stabilized, the governments of France, Poland, and Czechoslovakia stopped funding Savinkov. An appeal to Mussolini, whom Savinkov went to see in Rome, failed to elicit funds (instead, Mussolini gave him a batch of Italian passports). Savinkov was forced to rely almost exclusively on private donors, such as Reilly. By his own estimates, Reilly during 1920–1924 had poured £15,000–20,000 into the cause. But by 1924, he had little cash to spare.

Still, Reilly remained obsessed with the idea of overthrowing the Bolshevik government. Of course, as always with Reilly, it wasn't a purely ideological or "civilizational" drive. He calculated that Russian regime change could benefit him financially. But it was a Sisyphean struggle. By 1924, the Communists were well entrenched. They had won the civil war and largely crushed dissident voices. True, Lenin, the great leader and ideologue, had been greatly weakened by the 1918 assassination attempt and a succession of serious illnesses—he was working two hours or less a day in 1922, and in January 1924 he expired. But the regime remained robust. The Red Army had been fashioned into a large, professional military force, and the Cheka, since 1922 called the OGPU, was as omnipresent and omniscient as ever.

But Russian émigrés and right-wing groups abroad continued to plot. Reilly remained optimistic that the regime could be toppled. Its terrorization of the Russian population, while assuring automatic, short-term compliance, had, he believed, rendered it deeply unpopular. Moreover, Russia's economy remained precarious, with widespread food shortages, even hunger, and with the development of industry impeded by lack of investments, spare parts, and foreign markets. The economic debacle was partly fueled by Russia's continued international ostracism, meaning that its economy was effectively laboring under sanctions. And by 1923, the Leninist-Trotskyist dream of exporting revolution, especially to central Western Europe, had fizzled out, with the handful of "pink" or Red postwar regimes that had taken power being swiftly overthrown (*vide* Bavaria, Hungary). Most of the world remained resistant to the lure of Bolshevism and the Communist International.

Reilly put his faith in Savinkov. Pepita may not have been able to fathom why his followers, including her Reilly, "idolised" the man. But for Reilly, Savinkov, despite his morphine addiction, was the man who would serve as the figurehead if not the actual leader and orchestrator of the counterrevolution. In the end, he proved a giant disappointment and foolishly fell victim to a Cheka counterplot.

Back in 1921 or 1922, the Cheka/OGPU had clandestinely set up a fake anti-Soviet underground organization called the Monarchist Union of Central Russia, commonly referred to as "the Trust." Leading the operation was Alexander Yakushev, who worked under Cheka counterintelligence head Artur K. Artuzov. The Cheka recruited a handful of former tsarist officers and turned them. They then recruited genuine counterrevolutionary leaders and operatives inside Russia and in Europe, who believed that they were working for a genuine anti-Bolshevik underground, with cohorts of sympathizers inside Russia, ready to storm the Kremlin once circumstances gelled. In fact, the whole underground, with its turned officers at the top and sincere anti-Bolshevik operatives on the ground, was run from Cheka's Moscow headquarters.

From the first, one of the Chekists' main targets was Savinkov, and for much of 1923–1924 the puppet masters in the Kremlin labored to either kill or kidnap him in Warsaw or Paris and lure him back to Russia, where he could be tried and executed. With this end in mind, the Trust managed to recruit and turn Savinkov's aides, L. D. Sheshenya and M. D. Zekunov; they also deployed OGPU officers A. P. Fyodorov and Eduard Ottovich Opperput to pose as anti-Bolsheviks.

In 1924, Savinkov was at last persuaded by these conspirators to return to Russia, there purportedly to organize the anti-Bolshevik underground for a *coup de main* that would topple the regime. The Chekists were aided by Savinkov's gnawing desire to put an end to his existence as a penurious exile and return to mother Russia. He probably half-sensed that he was walking into a trap. At a last-minute meeting in Paris, Reilly tried to dissuade him from going. But Savinkov refused to listen. His desire to return to the motherland—or perhaps it was a death wish—overcame natural caution. In the end, perhaps it was love, or at least lust, that sealed his fate.

By summer 1924, Lioubov Derental, the wife of his secretary Baron Derental, had become Savinkov's mistress. Savinkov was infatuated, and the Cheka found out. Lioubov, whom Reilly later called "a dirty stinking Jewess, with a shiny face, [and] fat hands and thighs," was recruited, with an offer of $5,000 if she could lure him to Russia. She demanded, and got, the Cheka payment up front.

On August 10, Savinkov, accompanied by both Derentals, entrained for Berlin, where he was met by Yakushev and Opperput, who gave him a fake Russian passport. On August 20, the whole party crossed into Belarus, on foot, in drenching rain. They were met by OGPU agents, possibly including Artuzov himself, pretending to be counterrevolutionaries. The group reached a forester's hut outside Minsk. Lioubov put the tea on the stove and began preparing an omelette. The OGPU officers abruptly announced themselves and disarmed the threesome, including Lioubov, who had a small pearl-handled Browning tucked into her underwear. She then said: "Gentlemen, please take your seats, the omelette is getting cold." The group ate up, with little or no conversation. According to the subsequent OGPU report, found in the KGB/NKVD archive, eye contact between the trappers and the entrapped was avoided.

After a short rest, Savinkov was driven to Minsk, and from

there the prisoner and his keepers entrained for Moscow. He spent weeks under interrogation, some of it by Cheka founder Dzerzhinsky himself. Dzerzhinsky tried to persuade Savinkov that the reality of Bolshevik Russia was far different from what he had imagined in Paris and Warsaw: The factories worked, there were no breadlines, the streets were clean, schools and universities ran smoothly. There were no teeming, seething, disaffected masses. Savinkov was even taken on a tour around Moscow to see for himself. Dzerzhinsky apparently offered him a deal: his life in exchange for a very public recantation.

Savinkov accepted. His trial, on August 27–29, was attended by journalists, including two from the West. Savinkov came off as a disenchanted idealist, a counterrevolutionary who had undergone a complete change of mind. The regime, he now agreed, had proven its durability and popularity. "I unconditionally recognize Soviet power and none besides. To every Russian who loves his country I, who have walked the paths of this bloody, serious, struggle against you, I who turned my back on you like none other, I say that if you are a Russian, if you love your people, you will bend down to worker-peasant power and recognize it without any reservations." Savinkov asked for the court's mercy, mercy for a man "who has never sought anything for himself and who devoted his whole life to the cause of the Russian people."

The mandatory death sentence was pronounced, but the judges promptly reduced it to ten years' imprisonment. No doubt it was all dictated by Stalin. Sent back to his comfortable cell in the Butyrka Inner Jail, Savinkov was allowed visits, even from his mistress, Madame Derental, who occasionally stayed the night.

Reilly and his counterrevolutionary colleagues abroad learned about what had happened from a report in the *Times* (London) on September 3. They were stunned and incredulous. The foremost leader of the anti-Bolshevik cause now openly supported the Bolshevik government? Reilly shot off a letter to London's *Morning Post* (with a copy to Churchill), which was published on September 8. He defended Savinkov's reputation and honor. He wrote that the Moscow proceedings were a "stunt" and a "fraud," and that Savinkov had died a few weeks before the "trial," while crossing into Russia; the man in the dock was an imposter, playing a role in a Cheka-organized show trial designed to undermine the counterrevolutionary cause.

But then came the follow-up reports in the Western and Russian press, and Reilly was forced to accept reality. On September 15, he published a second letter in the *Morning Post.* He admitted his "error," induced, he said, by his "loyalty to Savinkov." He denounced the man's "treachery," confirmed "beyond all possibility of doubt." Savinkov had "betrayed his friends, his organization, and his cause" and had gone over to "his former enemies," wrote Reilly. Savinkov had "dealt the heaviest possible blow at the anti-Bolshevik movement" and handed the Bolsheviks "an outstanding political triumph." "By this act Savinkov has erased forever his name from the scroll of honour of the anti-Communist movement," Reilly concluded, but he promised that he and his colleagues would "close ranks and carry on."

Churchill snapped off a letter to Reilly the same day: "I do not think that you should judge Savinkov too harshly. He was placed in a terrible position; and only those who have sustained successfully such an ordeal have a full right to pronounce censure. At any rate I shall wait to hear the end of the story before changing my view of Savinkov."

But the "end of the story" came more swiftly than many had anticipated. Within months, Stalin or Dzerzhinsky—or the full Communist Party Politburo—concluded that Savinkov's usefulness had come to an end. According to the version subsequently published by Moscow, on May 12 Savinkov jumped to his death from a fourth-floor prison window. But it is more likely that he was thrown to his death by OGPU officers.

Before his demise, Savinkov wrote a long, explanatory letter to Reilly, at the OGPU's diktat. Dated October 7, 1924, it stated: "You are one of the few people whom I not only love but whose opinion I value." The aim of the letter appears to have been threefold: to explain his actions to the world (he expected that the letter would be published), to persuade Reilly to give up his anti-Bolshevik hopes and activities, and to reach and persuade other counterrevolutionaries to change their hearts and ways. "Already in 1923 I came to the conclusion that it is impossible and perhaps unnecessary to struggle against the Bolsheviks," Savinkov wrote. "Impossible because we all (the Social Revolutionaries, the Mensheviks, the Constitutional Democrats, the Savinkovtzki and the rest) are definitely beaten . . . [and] the Russian people are not with us but with the Soviet Government." Even the peasants, now given land, were with the Bolsheviks. Similarly, the Bolsheviks had vastly improved the condition of Russia, economically and in other ways. "You abroad are still dreaming of 1918–1919; you still see the dried fish soup, the darkness, the looting, the executions, the typhus and the lice. All this does not exist anymore. In Russia there is order. The fields are sown and the sowing is increasing with every year. Industrial production is rising." Savinkov now acknowledged his "mistake."

Reilly was appalled. He wrote Spears that Savinkov was imprisoned "under the most comfortable circumstances" and "seems to spend his time chiefly in writing to his friends, attempting to justify his treachery, and generally in making propaganda for the Bolsheviks." He, Reilly, had been "honoured" with the longest letter, obviously written under Cheka "supervision and censorship." "Its hypocrisy, cynicism and callousness are equaled only by its length." He asked Spears to forward it, in translation, to Churchill and to Churchill's friend Archibald Sinclair, MP. Reilly averred that he was "more optimistic as regards impending doom of the Bolshevik regime than I ever was," basing himself on the alleged disaffection with the regime of the Russian peasantry.

Savinkov's fate no doubt reinforced Reilly's loathing for the Bolshevik regime. But now he had moved to the head of the OGPU's target list, either for assassination or abduction. According to Pepita, the OGPU tried to do just that in Paris in January 1924, when Russian agents, arriving on his doorstep, attempted to lure Reilly to come see her, saying that she had been hit by a car and was in hospital. But somehow Pepita—who was briefly in the agents' hands—managed to get away and warn Reilly before he set off for the hospital, thus frustrating the abductors' designs. If Pepita's story was true, then Reilly clearly had become a prize Soviet target.

In January 1924, just before the Paris abduction episode, the Soviets—using gullible Trust operatives—had tried nonviolently to lure Reilly back to Russia, in parallel with their efforts to lay hold of Savinkov. A "Mr. Warner" (later he admitted to the Russian name Drebkoff) showed up at Reilly's London flat and tried to persuade him to return to Russia to lead the anti-Bolshevik campaign. Warner was clearly not English, according to Pepita, and was gigantic, "his arms were long and huge as those of a great ape." He sported "a tremendous black beard" that "almost hid his face" and had "a pair of cold and steely blue eyes." He claimed that he headed "the White Russian organization in Moscow" and showed Reilly a "voucher" signed by Savinkov, whom he had met in Paris. He said he represented the whole underground movement. The movement, he said, needed "a man who can command and get things done . . . a man who will be master, dictator if you like, as Mussolini is in Italy." Drebkoff, according to Pepita's later account, related that "after your [Reilly's] last visit to us, hope died within us . . . we were leaderless." The movement, he said, had emerged from the ruins of Reilly's old 1918 network, and he named Reilly's old helpers, "Balkoff," "Tuenkoff," "Alvendorff," and "Vorislavsky" as figures in the resurrected underground. Drebkoff handed Reilly a (fake) Soviet passport. "As soon as you cross the border a million men will rally to your side," he said. "Come and be our leader."

Reilly was sorely tempted; the man had pressed all the right buttons. But Pepita, according to her memoir, intervened, saying that her man was "unwell" and couldn't make the arduous journey. And Reilly himself piped in: "What about Savinkoff? . . . The very man for you, a really great man." Drebkoff countered: "The people will not rally around Savinkoff as they would round you, Captain Reilly." But the Reillys stood their ground and Drebkoff went off, "dejectedly." The Reillys met Drebkoff at least twice more and were charmed by him (according to Pepita), but Reilly refused to commit to an immediate return to Russia, though he apparently left the door open for the future.

After their setback with Reilly, the OGPU pressed ahead with the Savinkov plot, landing the big counterrevolutionary fish a few weeks later.

The Savinkov affair may indirectly have pushed Reilly into involvement in what came to be known as the "Zinoviev Letter." Grigory Zinoviev (born Hirsch Apfelbaum), one of Lenin's closest associates, was simultaneously chairman of the Petrograd soviet and chairman of the Communist International (Comintern), the Bolshevik agency charged with uniting the world's Communist parties and exporting the proletarian revolution. Since August 1924, Zinoviev had been busy promoting or even orchestrating a campaign to undermine Britain's hold on India.

On October 8, 1924, the British Labour-led government fell in a vote of no confidence after the Liberal Party bolted the coalition over the government's handling of the alleged Communist threat to Britain. The "Red Menace" was the major issue in the election campaign that followed. On October 26, 1924, the *Daily Mail*, a Conservative newspaper, published a leaked translation of the text of what was alleged to be a letter by Zinoviev and news of an as yet undelivered British protest to Moscow concerning that letter. The article greatly embarrassed Labour's leaders. The letter, dated September 15 and addressed to the British Communist Party, urged the party to recruit followers in the British armed forces and to spread "Leninism in England and the Colonies." Zinoviev promised Soviet assistance in these subversive activities.

Britain was in the grip of election fever. The Conservatives charged that the government's nonpublication of the letter—it had been in government hands since October 9 or 10—and the failure to take Moscow to task over it was an act of appeasement, or worse, and painted Labour's leader Ramsay MacDonald as a pinko, a closet Communist sympathizer. It was unclear then, and remains unclear to this day, whether the letter was genuine. But its publication and the brouhaha around it helped bring about MacDonald's defeat in the October 29 general elections, which were followed by the return of the Conservatives to power.

The letter, or an English translation of it, probably originating in Riga, had been in SIS hands since the start of October and was likely leaked to the *Daily Mail* by serving or former British intelligence officers or the Conservative Central Office. It appears that the letter was concocted by anti-Bolshevik Russians in Reval on the basis of real letters and statements made by Zinoviev at the time. It is possible that Reilly had a hand in the concoction, or at least in the letter's transmission to the Conservative Party or the *Daily Mail* (as some British newspapers alleged after his death). The publication of the letter days before the election helped generate anti-Soviet sentiment and may have helped the Conservatives, if only marginally, win by the landslide that followed.

8

Last Days

IT IS SOMEWHAT STRANGE, in retrospect, that Savinkov's arrest and trial failed to dent the belief among Russian expatriates that the Trust was a real, powerful, and active counterrevolutionary organization. Nor, it appears, was British intelligence put on its guard. Indeed, the SIS station chief in Helsinki, Commander Ernest Boyce, responsible for operations in the Baltic, in January 1925 began to sound out Reilly about going to Russia to probe the Trust's capabilities—just as Reilly himself was mulling over the idea. Boyce was taken in principally by Maria Zakhavchenko-Shultz, the daughter of a tsarist colonel and a former fighter in Denikin's army, who worked as a Savinkov network courier. Sometime in 1924 she had turned coat and become an OGPU agent. Artuzov called Shultz, who was tasked to reel in Reilly, "the Sorceress."

Boyce sent Reilly a coded letter, couched as a business-manufacturing proposition. He hinted that the approach was a personal initiative, not on orders from London ("keep our connection with this business from the knowledge of my department," he wrote). Reilly responded in a series of letters during March–April 1925, equally coded. On March 25, Reilly wrote that he was "51 yesterday and I want to do something worthwhile whilst I can. All the rest does not matter." On April 4, writing from New York City, he gave a definite answer, almost *en clair:* "I fully agree with the Board that the simplest and most direct way to gather all the necessary data and to arrive at a complete understanding as to future operations and improvements of manufacture is for me to come out and to inspect the factory personally. . . . I am prepared to come out as soon as I have arranged my affairs here."

In September, after Reilly's return to Europe, Boyce met up with him (and Pepita) in Paris, probably at Maxim's. Pepita subsequently traveled to Ostend to visit her mother while Reilly had meetings with various Russian expatriates, to take advice about the Trust and a possible meeting with its leaders. On her return, Reilly told Pepita that he was "convinced of the sincerity and potentiality of this anti-Bolshevik organization." One of Reilly's contacts, General Alexander Kutyepov, a former White Russian commander (who later, in 1930, was kidnapped on a Paris street by OGPU agents and apparently died of a heart attack), cautioned Reilly that if he was going to meet Trust people, he should do so on the Finnish side of the Russian border and on no account cross into Russia, which would be "very dangerous."

The day before they departed—Reilly to Finland via Berlin and Pepita to Hamburg, there to await his return—"a small dapper man" dashed in front of them as they were leaving their hotel and snapped a picture of the couple. He then jumped into a taxi and sped away. The Reillys thought nothing of it in the moment. But later, Pepita came to view the incident as ominous. Reilly had assured her that he would not cross into Russia, yet, as they parted at the train station, she had "a feeling of impending calamity," she later wrote. "A whistle shrilled. I felt Sidney suddenly lift me into his arms. Then he set me down and stepped into the train." They were never to see each other again. "A lump rose in my throat. I suddenly wanted to cry. . . . The train had swept Sidney out of my life forever."

From Berlin Sidney wrote to Pepita: "I shall . . . take great care of myself . . . All the rest is on the knees of the Gods." Then from Helsinki: "I had a very rotten trip . . . I was not seasick but felt very headachy and congested." In the Finnish capital he was hosted by Nikolai Bunakov, one of Boyce's agents, codenamed ST28, a former Russian naval officer: "The piroshki were a dream," Reilly wrote, "and I longed to put a couple into my pocket and bring them home to you. Mrs. Bunakoff is also a dream, but a bad one. Enormous, elephantine female with peroxidized bobbed hair, black eyebrows and eyes like hot house plums, silly as a boot, absolutely ignorant as regards politics, but otherwise harmless and of course most hospitable. How perfectly normal and sane men get hold of *such* life companions is the greatest puzzle to me. (I must try and make a limerick on this subject.)"

From Helsinki, per his arrangement with the Trust agents, Reilly, accompanied by Shultz, traveled to Vyborg (Viipuri) on the Finnish side of the border, where he was to meet the Russian heads of the organization. Two OGPU agents, posing as Trust operatives, Alexander Yakushev and George Syroezhkin, were waiting. Reilly knew Yakushev from his days in Petrograd in 1917. But the Trust leaders were nowhere to be seen. Yakushev and Syroezhkin explained that the Trust's leaders, for a variety of reasons, could not come to Finland and that he must cross into Russia and look over the Trust operation personally.

Yakushev later recorded his first impression of Reilly: He was "unpleasant. His bulging dark eyes expressed something biting and cruel; his lower lip drooped deeply and he was too slick—the neat black hair, the demonstratively elegant suit. . . .

[Reilly] took a seat in an armchair, carefully adjusted the crease in his trousers, then showed off his new yellow shoes and silk stockings. He began the conversation with world-weary seriousness and a superior tone." The two Trust/OGPU operatives pressed him to cross the border.

Reilly penned one last letter to Pepita, from Vyborg, dated September 25. He left it in Bunakov's care, to be handed to Pepita in the event that he did not return. A few weeks later, Bunakov reached Paris and handed it to her. It read: "My most beloved, my sweetheart, it is absolutely necessary that I should go for three days to St. Petersburg and Moscow . . . I want you to know that I would not have undertaken this trip unless it was absolutely essential, and if I was not convinced that there is *practically no* risk attached to it. . . . I am doing what I must do . . . You are in my thoughts always . . . I love you beyond all words. Sidney." Though nothing is explicit, one senses that Reilly was apprehensive.

Accompanied by his duplicitous OGPU chaperones, Reilly crossed into Russia on the night of September 25/26. Boyce later cabled SIS HQ that Reilly had gone into Russia against his advice. It is unclear whether Boyce had informed SIS in advance that Reilly was infiltrating into Russia. Crossing the border just south of Vyborg, Reilly and his party encountered no Soviet patrols. "We walked slowly, ear attuned to every little whisper," Yakushev later wrote in his report. "Reilly's new boots squeaked so we . . . dug little holes in them with a knife. . . . Crossing the [Sestro] River took considerable time because Reilly, in addition to undressing and dressing, had to unwind and then rewind the elastic bandages he wore for the swollen veins in his legs. In pouring rain we approached Peschanoi Station. . . . Then we took the first train to Leningrad [St. Petersburg]."

There, in Syroezhkin's flat, Reilly was introduced to a "[supposed] member of the Moscow Municipal Council [and Trust leader]," Vladimir Styrne, who was, in fact, deputy head of the

OGPU's counterintelligence department. The OGPU agents continued with their pretense. Styrne filled Reilly in with supposed details about the Trust. In the evening, accompanied by Yakushev and another imposter, Reilly entrained for Moscow. The three discussed Savinkov and his poor judgment about people and his dissolute habits—women and gambling. According to Yakushev, they also talked about "the Jews." He later quoted Reilly (who was code-named "KAN" in Yakushev's report) as saying that pogroms were unavoidable, given "popular feeling" in Russia. The Trust, once in power, should not itself sponsor pogroms but rather should say that pogroms were "a [true] expression of national feeling," Reilly suggested. But identifying with the pogroms would alienate people in the West, especially as the British and French financial firms were "completely in the hands of the Jews," he said, according to Yakushev, as was "a third" of the American economy. (Years later, Margaret Reilly was to recall that her husband once said that in post-Bolshevik Russia, the country would be entering its "convalescent stage, when she would turn round and massacre at least one million Jews." In other words, according to Margaret, Reilly anticipated that after the overthrow of the Bolshevik regime, there would be a popular payback given the prominence of Jews in the Bolshevik-Cheka hierarchy.)

Arriving in Moscow, Reilly—outside a church—knelt and crossed himself, according to Yakushev's report. Reilly was then taken to a dacha in Malakhovka, outside the city, where he met the Trust's ostensible leaders. They had just eaten and assembled under a tree. The game was still on. Reilly expounded on the organization's financial problem. The foreign powers, Britain included, were no longer willing to invest in counterrevolution in Russia. The Trust must raise its own funds. He then expanded on his museum-raiding proposal, previously described to Yakushev: that Trust operatives break into and rob Russian museum storerooms. Reilly mentioned specific paintings and antiques to target. He said the treasures should then be smuggled to the West and that he, Reilly, would handle the sales. He promised to raise the $50,000 needed to carry out this campaign of museum robberies, and brushed aside as "useless sentimentality" objections that this might tarnish the Trust's name. One can only speculate that his OGPU-cum-Trust audience regarded the idea—to denude Russia of its cultural treasures—as yet another in the capitalist con man Reilly's money-making schemes. It is worth noting that General Spears in 1967 told Bruce Lockhart that he believed Reilly had gone back to Russia in 1925 "in search of a valuable collection of coins and Napoleonic relics which he said he wanted to retrieve"—in addition to his counterrevolutionary hopes and aims.

From the dacha, Reilly was driven back to Moscow, where he assumed he would be boarding the train for Leningrad on the first leg of his journey back to Vyborg. Instead, his companions overpowered and handcuffed him, and then drove him straight to the Lubyanka, the OGPU headquarters, a former insurance company building. Reilly was "welcomed" by senior officer Roman Pilar, the same officer who the year before had arrested Savinkov. Pilar casually mentioned that Reilly was still under the 1918 death sentence. A cursory interrogation followed. Reilly identified himself but refused to name fellow British agents. He was then taken to cell number 73. In his remaining days, Reilly would be known as "Prisoner 73."

Meanwhile, OGPU operatives staged a shooting incident on the Russian side of the border with Finland, near Vyborg, and a Soviet truck then took away "two bodies." The anti-Bolshevik Trust operatives in Moscow were informed that Reilly had been shot. Word eventually reached MI6 in London, though for weeks a desperate Pepita was left in the dark about her husband's fate. "I knew nothing, I was ignorant," she recalled. She traveled to London and waylaid Boyce over breakfast. Boyce told her that

Reilly had been badly injured at the border, but that nothing more was known. Moscow was saying nothing. "I was like a caged lion," she recalled. She decided to go to Helsinki and meet Maria Shultz, Reilly's Trust contact. Shultz told Pepita what had happened and implicitly confirmed that Reilly had been fatally wounded.

Pepita returned to Paris and informed the *Times* (London) of her husband's death. The paper duly published a notice on December 15, 1925, informing its readers that Captain Sidney Reilly had been killed on September 28 by Soviet security men on the Finnish border.

But of course, Reilly was still alive after September 28. He was interrogated, probably in English, by Styrne on October 7. Throughout his interrogations, Reilly was never physically tortured. Indeed, for most of his incarceration, in a cell by himself, he seems to have lived in relative comfort. Strangely, Styrne, in his report on the interrogation, recorded that Reilly was born in Clonmel, Ireland, to a British sea captain and a Russian mother (presumably Styrne was simply writing down what Reilly told him)—though since their investigation of the "Lockhart Plot," the Cheka knew that Reilly was Russian, and probably Jewish to boot. Reilly was forthcoming about some of his history, including his MI6 service during 1918–1921 and his "fight against Soviet power." Also, at Styrne's request, Reilly wrote a statement about his part in the 1918 plot, his escape from Russia, his subsequent work in southern Russia, and his meetings in Paris during the peace conference. The statement included information about his first contacts with Savinkov. Reilly may have offered to work for the OGPU/KGB under certain conditions, but if so, his offer was rejected.

During these interrogation sessions, the OGPU forced Reilly to witness the execution of a fellow inmate. But he remained steadfast in his unwillingness to implicate anyone else in espionage or subversion—that is, to spill the beans about his British intelligence or Russian counterrevolutionary contacts. The interrogation stretched into weeks.

Toward the end, Reilly kept a sort of diary, written in minute English or Cyrillic characters on small bits of paper, covering the period October 30–November 4. These were later collected, magnified, and deciphered by the OGPU. According to the diary, on October 30 Styrne threatened Reilly with immediate execution "unless he agreed to cooperate." Reilly responded that he was "ready to die." Styrne gave him an hour to reconsider and sent him back to his cell. Reilly "prayed inwardly for P[ep]ita, made [a] small package of [his] personal things, smoked a couple of cigarettes and after fifteen or twenty minutes said [he] was ready [to die]." The interrogators left him to simmer for another hour, then he was hauled back to face Styrne. Reilly repeated his decision and asked to make a written declaration—"to show them how an Englishman and a Christian understands his duty." The Soviets refused, and said that his death would not be reported or described to the outside world. After some further "wrangling," Styrne called in the executioner, one Ibrahim Abisalov, and Reilly was handcuffed and taken outside. The guards made a show of priming their weapons. But no execution ensued. Instead, Reilly was stuffed into a car and driven around Moscow. He recorded that a "soldier squeezed his filthy hands between [the] handcuffs and my wrist." The car then halted in a garage. Reilly again thought he was about to be executed. But he was then driven back to the Lubyanka and told that a twenty-hour stay of execution had been ordered. "Terrible night. Nightmares," he recorded. The OGPU officers, for their part, later reported that Reilly spent the night alternately "crying and praying before a small picture of Pepita."

But the mock (pre-)execution had done the trick. That day, October 30, Reilly sent Dzerzhinsky a letter (though some have since maintained that the letter is an OGPU forgery) agreeing to "cooperate in sincerely providing full evidence and information," including about British fellow agents, American intelligence, and Russian émigré organizations. It is probable that Reilly had no intention of spilling all the beans but saw the letter—if he indeed penned it—as a way of buying time or even completely neutering the threat of execution.

Be that as it may, during the following days Reilly provided the OGPU with information—about British intelligence, about sundry British figures such as Churchill and Spears, and about Russian émigré counterrevolutionaries. But most, if not all, of it was low-grade and likely already known to the OGPU. Reilly said nothing, and perhaps had nothing to say, about current British intelligence operatives in Russia ("ignorance of any agents here," he succinctly penned in his diary). On October 31 he was treated to a feast ("a great spread") outside the Lubyanka, somewhere in Moscow. Then he was driven back to his cell. During the following days he was frequently taken for walks in parks around Moscow.

Styrne informed Reilly that Moscow had "stopped" or suspended his death sentence, but he was continuously interrogated—about 1918, the SIS and its operatives, British politics, the "American secret service," American banks and politics, Russian émigrés, including Savinkov, and British agents in the Comintern and Petrograd, including counterrevolutionaries who had become OGPU agents (Ilya Kurtz, Alexei Stark, Eduard Opperput, and Sergei Ivanovich Kheidulin). The interrogations were subsequently summarized in written reports by Styrne and others. Reilly was once again subjected to a meager diet and poor living conditions. Genrikh Yagoda, the OGPU's number three, took part in the questioning. Reilly recorded on November 2–4: "Getting very weak. Hungry all day. . . . Very weak." He appeared to believe that the death sentence had indeed been revoked, but he had trouble sleeping and frequently took Veronal. "I stopped worrying about my death," he recorded.

Over the years since 1925 the idea has persisted that Reilly was not executed but, switching loyalties, had enlisted with the Communists, and for the next two decades, served the OGPU-NKVD-KGB as an expert on Britain and the West, even indirectly training agents run by the Soviets in Britain, including the Cambridge "moles" of the 1930s–1950s, Kim Philby, Donald McLean, Guy Burgess, and Antony Blunt.

This notion was partly based on the suspicion, voiced by, among others, American diplomats and SIS officers as early as 1918, that Reilly was in fact a Bolshevik agent or sympathizer. The notion was enhanced by a succession of reported "sightings" of Reilly, or at least reports of his activities in Russia down to and during World War Two. Indeed, an entire book, Robin Bruce Lockhart's *Reilly: The First Man* (1987)—his second book on the spy—is devoted to "proving" that Reilly worked for the Soviets between 1925 and 1944 and was "important" in fashioning the NKVD/KGB during those years. Robin Lockhart even attributed the appointment in 1941 of George Hill, Reilly's fellow spy from 1918, as the SOE's liaison with the NKVD, to Reilly's influence on Lavrentiy Beria, the head of the NKVD during World War Two.

But neither Lockhart, nor any of Reilly's subsequent biographers, have offered firm evidence that Reilly ever worked for the Soviet government or intelligence arms, or that he lived beyond 1925. Rather, the available sources, including most prominently the available OGPU files, indicate that Reilly was executed on November 5, 1925.

By November 4 the Russians had concluded that Reilly had been squeezed dry and was expendable, and decided to renege on the mooted agreement positing Reilly's cooperation in exchange for his life. The order to execute him came from Dzerzhinsky or Stalin himself, though there were some OGPU officers who preferred that Reilly be kept alive. They argued that it was best to adhere to the fiction of Reilly's unintended death in a border skirmish so that no one would suspect the Trust's duplicity, and perhaps they believed that Reilly could be traded for someone valuable down the road.

Nonetheless, the execution went ahead. On November 5, Reilly was taken on one of his routine outings, probably to Sokolniki Park. The agent in charge of the execution, Grigory Feduleev, of the fourth section of the KRO, the OGPU's counterintelligence department, later reported:

> Comrades Dukis, Syroezhkin, myself, and Ibrahim drove out of the OGPU yard with No. 73. . . . We set out toward Bogorodsk. . . . It was agreed that the driver, when we got to the [designated] spot, would [stop and] repair a "fault" in the car, which he did. . . . I then proposed to No. 73 that we stretch our legs. When we had gone thirty or forty paces from the car Ibrahim, who had dropped back, fired a shot at No. 73, who let out a deep gasp and fell to the ground without uttering a word. His heart was still beating, [so] Comrade Syroezhkin fired a shot into his chest. After waiting a little longer, ten to fifteen minutes, the pulse finally stopped beating, and we carried him to the car and drove straight to the medical unit, where Comrade Kushner and the photographer were already waiting. . . . The four of us carried No. 73 into the building indicated by Comrade Kushner. We told the orderly that this person had been hit by a tram. His face could not be seen as the head was in a sack, and [we] put him on the dissecting table. . . . He was photographed down to the waist in a greatcoat, then naked down to the waist so that the wounds could be seen, then naked full length. After this he was placed in a sack and taken to the morgue next to the Medical Unit, where he was put in a coffin and we all went home. The whole operation was completed by 11:00 p.m. on 5 November. No. 73 was collected from the morgue of the OGPU medical unit by Com. Dukis at 8:30 p.m. on 9 November 1925 and driven to the prepared burial pit in the walking yard of the OGPU inner prison, where he was put

in a sack so that the 3rd Red Army men burying him could not see his face.

On June 8, 1927, Moscow officially announced Reilly's death as having occurred in the "summer of 1925."

The publication in the British press in December 1925 of Reilly's death stirred great public interest. Of course, the event itself—a former British intelligence officer killed in Russia—was dramatic and newsworthy. But Reilly was already in the British public eye, due to the spate of news reports two years before announcing his marriage to the "beautiful" actress Pepita Bobadilla. Those reports had been studded both with hyperbole and praise of "our man in Berlin and Moscow," and had turned him overnight into the most publicized British intelligence agent of his day. For example, the provincial Sunday paper the *Empire News*, on May 20, 1923, two days after the marriage, reported that Reilly during World War One had "penetrated into the very heart of Germany, obtaining the most valuable information . . . and passing on 'dud' information in return." Afterward, he had traveled to Russia "determined to use whatever powers he possessed to help overthrow the Bolshevik reign of terror. . . . The gallant captain . . . posed as one of the most fanatical Bolsheviks alive, and so revolutionary were his utterances . . . that he became a very important official in the Soviet organization, being recognized by all the Commissars as 'Comrade R.' . . . He was admitted to the [Russians'] secret conclaves." Later, his real identity uncovered, he "made a bold [successful] dash for liberty" through Finland.

The news stories following Reilly's death that appeared in the *Daily News* and *Daily Express* of December 16 and 17, 1925—accompanied by a photograph of Reilly and Pepita—attached to Reilly more than a hint of glamour. Here was an early James Bond, as it were.

The news reports triggered a spate of inquiries by both Pepita and Margaret about Reilly's fate. Margaret's letter of February 25, 1926, to the British embassy in Brussels also alluded to herself as being "absolutely without means." She clearly was seeking a British government widow's pension or grant. The Foreign Office Northern Department brushed this off (March 12, 1926) with "there is no fund from which HMG could give her any financial assistance." At some point thereafter Margaret tried to commit suicide with a pistol shot.

By 1931, Margaret was working in Brussels as a governess and renewed her representations to the British government, this time suggesting that her husband might still be "alive and safe" in Russia. She "threatened" to come in person to the War Office. C—Hugh "Quex" Sinclair, Cumming's successor—was at first "averse" to British officials agreeing to meet her. But Sinclair's aides "pointed out that if she was not seen she would probably go to MPs or the Press and make a fuss." So C was persuaded, but said that she was to be told that Reilly had not been working for the government since 1921 and had gone off to Russia and his death "entirely on his own." Moreover, Margaret should not be "promised anything at all."

Meanwhile, Pepita contacted the Russian authorities with a view to getting them to issue a death certificate that would enable her to remarry. She also periodically appealed to the British government for money, but to no avail. A decade or so after Reilly's passing, at the start of World War Two, Pepita Bobadilla (once again calling herself Pepita Haddon Chambers), short of funds or out of patriotism, tried to enlist in MI6 (or join the Foreign Office). "I speak fluent German, Dutch and French, also know the different dialects [such] as Flemish etc. [And] I can type in a poor way." She added that she had done "anti-Communist work" during the previous decades. "Consequently am used to doing espionage work. I also worked in conjunction with the French Police in their anti-Bolshevik work. . . .

I am a . . . reliable worker and am willing to do anything." But "her offers of service were declined," recorded an MI6 officer in 1944. She apparently died in London in 1974, an obscure alcoholic.

And then there was Caryll Houselander, the young artist who became a Catholic mystic. Years later, while visiting Germany, she jotted down in her diary: "There is a man here who has a note in his voice like Sidney. . . . I am obliged to talk to him often and it twists my heart to do so. After all these years of driving back the thought of Sidney, I am still so weak that I cannot see the faintest likeness of him in anyone without feeling as if my whole life is an open wound." Caryll began to call herself Sidonie, later shortened to Sid.

She died in 1954. But two and a half decades earlier, in 1930, she published a poem entitled "To SGR Killed in Russia" in a British Catholic periodical, *The Messenger of the Sacred Heart*, in which she compared (some might say inappropriately) Reilly's death—"this later calvary"—to the passion and martyrdom of another Jew, Jesus of Nazareth. Reilly would have enjoyed that.

A Look Back—and Forward

Sidney Reilly, perhaps the twentieth century's most famous spy, and certainly its most famous Jewish spy, would never have been hired as a case officer by the Mossad, Israel's foreign intelligence service. Neither, probably, would they have hired James Bond.

Over the years, writers have spoken of the two in the same breath. And though they shared one or two characteristics, Reilly and Bond were entirely different kettles of fish. Both dressed impeccably, had good manners, and passed (most of the time) for gentlemen. But both came from ungenteel backgrounds: Reilly was clearly a "foreigner," a lowly category in the eyes of most Britons, and Bond had a vaguely working-class smell about him (as Vesper Lynd points out in the film *Casino Royale*). And both clearly did not lack for money. Bond, certainly as portrayed initially (and best) by Sean Connery, was tall, dark, and very handsome; Reilly was short, dark, and unprepossessing, to judge from contemporary descriptions and photos. But both were irresistible to women. It was partly due to charm. In Bond's—Connery's—case, the charm was complemented by a dominant physicality. Reilly's sex appeal is less fathomable. Women said they were immediately struck by his air of mystery and adventure. But as with Bond, there was clearly something deeper at work: both men clearly toyed with death as a way of life.

John le Carré once wrote of Kim Philby, the famous KGB mole in Britain's intelligence services, that he ran the gamut of disloyalties—to his country, his friends, and his wives. Reilly (and Bond) were different. Both were loyal Britons, one might even say patriots, while, at the same time, serially disloyal, or unfaithful, to their women. Reilly bedded, occasionally wedded, and, in short order, dumped them, while Bond bedded, never (or at most once) came close to saying "I do," and moved on to the next one in fairly short order. Reilly, like Bond, was the antithesis of a family man; as far as we know, he had no children and presumably wanted none. Through his adult life he flitted like a bee, from flower to flower (albeit flowers that beckoned him).

But Bond and Reilly were essentially different creatures. Reilly, however sociable and smooth, was a loner for most of his life, a free agent. As a spy and political conspirator he was a pieceworker: he carried out specific tasks for Melville (though Melville may have paid him a small monthly retainer) and did as he pleased in the anti-Bolshevik cause. Only during 1918–1921 was Reilly a full-time employee of a state intelligence agency, MI6. Bond, on the other hand, from the moment we get to know him, in print and on screen, is a full-time MI6 operative, all expenses paid, pension guaranteed. Bond may occasionally skirt or disobey orders and dis his superiors, but he is no maverick; he works for the company and does what he is told. He is in and of the establishment.

But truth be told, Bond is not really much of a spy; indeed, he is no spy at all. As 007, he spends most of his professional time hunting down and killing Her Majesty's or personal enemies, not gathering intelligence, which is what spies actually do. Reilly may have killed a few people along his way, apparently for personal gain, but he spent most of his spying days gathering intelligence and sending in reports—which admixed raw intelligence, political-economic analysis, and, unusually, advice—as he did from Russia during 1918–1919. One cannot picture Bond writing a report, and the intelligence he occasionally gathers is purely tactical, dedicated to facilitating his next hit.

So how successful was Reilly the spy? Well, in the years preceding his dismissal from MI6, he had dramatically failed to topple the Bolshevik regime, and there may have been other, lesser failures. And no doubt his extravagant and dissolute lifestyle, his dubious commercial antics, and his occasional displays of indiscipline and manipulativeness were all there in MI6's negative collective memory of the man, as were his presumed Jewish origins (before the 1930s, MI6 had almost no Jewish officers).

But over the years Reilly had actually chalked up a string of successes beneficial to Britain's security and to its understanding of international realities. In the years before World War One Reilly had fed Britain's internal security apparatus, such as it was, with information on potentially troublesome Russian revolutionaries living in London and Paris, and he helped London keep abreast of German armaments production. He also provided London with intelligence about the tsarist army and navy. In Russia in the spring and summer of 1918 he certainly set up successful networks that gathered intelligence, and in the winter of 1918/1919, against the backdrop of the civil war, he fed Whitehall with fine appreciations and analyses of the changing geopolitics of southern Russia. And even Reilly's most spectacular failure—to topple Lenin and Trotsky in 1918—demonstrated his daring, capabilities, and vision. All these should also have been taken into account when MI6, after 1925, assessed Reilly's "legacy."

One can only speculate about how important a factor in Reilly's faltering career were his assumed Jewish origins. Less conjectural is Reilly's attitude to his Jewishness and Jewish background. He apparently never told any of his professional colleagues (C, George Hill, Thwaites) that he was Jewish—though they all assumed as much. For sure, Melville did, certainly after helping him change his name from Sigmund Rosenblum to Sidney Reilly. Later, the senior Cheka officer who interrogated Reilly in Moscow in 1925, Vladimir Styrne, recorded that Reilly "was extremely bothered by being a Jew and made every attempt to conceal his origin." Even under strenuous interrogation, he stuck to the fictions of his Irish birth and his British/Irish sea captain father.

We don't know if Reilly's abandonment of his Jewish identity and the name change induced any pangs of conscience or anguish; no such traces exist. What we do know is that after becoming "Sidney Reilly," he seems never to have looked back or displayed signs of remorse or ill-adjustment to his new, Christian (and Irish) identity. In 1916 he married his second or third wife, Nadine, in a Christian Orthodox cathedral; and on his (final) return to Russia in 1925 he was recorded as exhibiting respect if not reverence outside a Moscow church. Earlier, in 1919 in Odessa, he displayed in front of his fellow agent George Hill a moment of weakness when he halted by a house he recognized from his childhood or youth. But that was it. He appears not to have maintained contact with his family, save with his first cousin, Felicia Rosenblum, after his departure from Odessa almost three decades before. Clearly, he wished to distance himself from "the Odessa Jew-boy" (as some Russian bankers reportedly later referred to him), from the humiliating status of abasement and victimhood that was the lot of the Jew in the tsarist empire.

Becoming a British subject and gentleman was the ultimate negation of lowly, foreign Jewish origins. His choice of women, too, from Margaret Thomas to Anne Luke to Caryll Houselander to Pepita Bobadilla, certainly reflected this. Nadine Massino, who appears to have been of Jewish origin, was an exception— but her parents had converted to Christianity before she was born or just after, and she had been brought up a Christian.

During his years in London and working as Melville's agent among Russian exiles, Reilly may have abjured contact with Jews. But many of his later business partners and associates (Moisei Ginsburg, Alexandre Weinstein) in Russia, the Far East, and the United States were Jews. This, likely, was no reflection on Reilly's taste in friends but rather of the roles—middlemen and deal-abettors—Jews played in the business world. Curiously, it was Reilly's lot in Moscow and Petrograd in 1918, and again in 1925, to have been in close contact with a host of Jews when facing the Bolshevik establishment and the Cheka—where Jews, who had been prominent in anti-tsarist revolutionary circles, figured prominently (Litvinov, Trotsky, Jacob Peters, even one of Lenin's grandparents, Israel Blank, were Jewish). It is possible that Reilly's bone-deep anti-Bolshevism was in part due to the prevalence of Jews in the Soviet establishment—though of course, it was the Bolsheviks' anticapitalist ideology and terroristic praxis, contrary to Reilly's free-thinking, capitalist outlook, that lay at the heart of his anti-Communism.

Throughout his adult career, insofar as the accessible documents show, Reilly displayed deliberate, and surprising, indifference to the fate of his fellow Eastern European Jews. We have found no evidence of his response to the anti-Semitism he encountered as he grew up in Odessa, and in his reports from southern Russia in 1918–1919 he seems completely oblivious to the butchery that Jews were periodically being subjected to by both White and Red forces as well as Ukrainian nationalists. By radical contrast, the non-Jewish George Hill, Reilly's fellow

MI6 officer, repeatedly referred to the ongoing pogroms in his reports to London. Indeed, Reilly seems to have gone out of his way in his communications with MI6 to emphasize the pro-German—hence, anti-Allied and anti-British—attitudes of south Russia's Jews and their assistance to France when French and British interests, as in Odessa in early 1919, collided. Reilly repeatedly singled out for vilification promiscuous or (in his eyes) "ugly" Jewish women. Years later, in 1925, according to Cheka reports, when told of the possibility of the outbreak of massive anti-Jewish pogroms should the Bolshevik regime go under, Reilly seemed chiefly interested in the deflection of blame away from his counterrevolutionary colleagues rather than in their prevention.

The contrast on this score between Reilly and his fellow Odessan and Jew, Leon Trotsky—they were born some five years apart—is stark. Trotsky, like Reilly, had grown up in a largely unobservant Jewish home but had briefly attended *cheder* and learned a bit of Hebrew. For Trotsky, anti-Semitism was at least a minor underlying cause of his opposition to the tsarist regime as he matured into an active revolutionary. He was always keenly sensitive to the anti-Semitism prevalent in Russia, both before and after 1917. In his career as a socialist pamphleteer Trotsky repeatedly wrote about and condemned anti-Semitism, including during the Beilis trial. Once in power, in St. Petersburg (briefly) during the Revolution of 1905, and again after October 1917, Trotsky condemned and reportedly prevented pogroms.

Like Reilly, Trotsky in adulthood discarded his Jewish birth name (Lev Davidovich Bronstein). But in Reilly's case, the name change appears to have been prompted more by a desire to erase his origins than for practical career reasons—whereas Bronstein adopted the nom de guerre Trotsky mainly to avoid identification or capture by the Okhrana (a practice, incidentally, adopted by most of his fellow revolutionaries, Jewish and non-Jewish alike—Ulyanov/Lenin, Dzhugashvili/Stalin, and so on). Trotsky distanced himself from Judaism and his personal Jewish origins as a matter of ideology, seeing salvation for the Jews, and an end to "the Jewish Problem" and anti-Semitism, as lying in assimilation and the triumph of the universalist socialist creed. At one point, in a meeting with a rabbi, he was quoted as saying, "I am not a Jew—I am a Marxist internationalist. I have nothing in common with Jewish things." Trotsky consistently opposed Jewish separatism, be it as expressed through Bundism or Zionism (he denounced the latter in 1904 as a "tragic mirage"); Jews would be "led out of the ghetto" by socialism.

Trotsky had, or thought he had, a universal solution to "the Jewish Problem." But, as we have seen, there is no evidence to show that Reilly ever thought about solving Europe's or Russia's "Jewish problem" (as distinct from solving his personal Jewish identity problem). During the decades following the wave of pogroms of the early 1880s, Russian Jews had in effect three courses open to them, three solutions to their existential predicament: assimilation, in the hope that over time life among the Gentile majority would get better (with many hoping to facilitate the change by joining assimilationist revolutionary parties, à la Trotsky); migration, especially to the liberal, tolerant West, primarily the United States, as some two million Jews did by 1914; or Jewish nationalism—that is, Zionism—believing that salvation for Europe's persecuted Jews would be found only through immigration to Palestine and the establishment there of a Jewish national home or state that would provide them with safety, equality, and prosperity.

In effect Reilly adopted the second option: he fled Russia, vilified the assimilationist revolutionary ideologies, and settled in the West. Though we have found no explicit reference by Reilly to Zionism, we can safely assume that he consciously foreswore that path too, and we have no knowledge at all of his opinion on the prospective reestablishment of Jewish sovereignty in the Promised Land. We can safely assume that he was aware of

Zionism as an ideology and movement and likely discussed the subject before or after abandoning Russia in the mid-1890s. We know that in Odessa in 1918–1919 he admired and met with Pinhas Rutenberg, and later tried to help him get a visa to Britain. ("Rutenberg was apparently whitewashed as a result of an MI1c [i.e., MI6] report by one Lieut. Reilly," wrote "D.A.H.," an MI6 officer, in 1922. Colonel Stewart Menzies, a senior MI6 officer, commented in this respect that "it would be quite wrong to place implicit reliance on anything that Reilly said.") Rutenberg, a Russian revolutionary who turned Zionist after 1917, was a major figure in the economic development of the Zionist enterprise in Palestine during the 1920s and 1930s, founding the Palestine Electricity Company—which today, as the Israel Electricity Corporation, provides Israel and the occupied territories with their electricity needs.

Despite all we know about him and much of the evidence outlined above, Reilly remains an enigmatic figure, both because the available sources are sparse and because the man was something of a chameleon, constantly changing identities, activities, and venues. But still, it is worth trying to define what can be seen as the core question: What made Reilly run? Stansfield Turner, a past director of the CIA, once described Reilly as "a man who sold himself to various governments and clearly gained satisfaction . . . from manipulating people and governments." "Sold himself to various governments" seems a bit strong—and certainly inapplicable to the mature Reilly, say after 1914. But he certainly appears to have been—like many spies have been—addicted to the nuts and bolts, the craft, of spying; he enjoyed knowing what the great masses out there didn't, hobnobbing with and claiming membership in a secret elite, living in the shadows, the danger and sexiness of the profession.

But Reilly clearly had other, overarching passions, and it would appear that they evolved, in staggered fashion, as he matured. After leaving Russia as a penniless youth, his primary ambition seems to have been to find a safe haven, cast off his Russian-Jewish identity, and establish himself as a genteel gentile in Western society. In 1895 he adopted Britain as the venue and never looked back, during the remainder of his life remaining faithful to his adopted homeland. Success in business was the main tool through which he hoped to attain, and to a degree did attain, social acceptance and recognition. Changing his name from Sigmund Rosenblum to Sidney Reilly both symbolized and advanced the goal. And marriage to a prosperous gentile Englishwoman (who was actually Irish) helped, as did his subsequent marriages.

In New York during the First World War, Reilly further advanced up the socioeconomic ladder by making piles of money. This had become his second passion. In 1917 he joined the British armed forces—the Royal Flying Corps—thus taking another step up the social ladder and in his transformation into an Englishman. Joining MI6 the following year meant entering the very heart of the British establishment (just as Kim Philby was to do, at least partly with the same purpose in mind, two decades later). But for Reilly, this proved insufficient. His colleagues and superiors all knew that he was no Englishman and suspected that he was, in origin, a Russian Jew. MI6, while recognizing his virtues as a secret agent, let him go as soon as it had no further use for him.

In the course of Reilly's social climb, however, history obtruded—and revolutionized and upgraded his ambitions. A third passion accrued. While still hankering for riches, the universal cataclysm that was the world war and his tangential involvement in it as a broker of arms to Russia whetted his appetite to play a role in history, a role for which the revolution in Russia provided, as it were, a natural venue.

From 1917 to 1918, borne on the wings of MI6 and the Russian Revolution, Reilly very consciously stepped onto the world stage. Most spies simply collect intelligence; very few actually

affect history or sense that they are participating in its forma-
tion. Reilly was different. Involved in counterrevolutionary subversion, Reilly began to see himself as the grand plotter, the
man who would organize and perhaps even lead regime change
and the restructuring of the world's largest state. In war-torn,
crisis-ridden Russia, anything seemed possible. In 1918, Reilly
set his mind to make his mark on history, a supremely ambitious denouement and apogee for an orphaned, poor, exiled
Jewish youngster. It would be the ultimate home-town-boy-
makes-good story.

Some who met Savinkov, Reilly's counterrevolutionary
friend and colleague, remarked on his constant pose, a hand
shoved into his waistcoat, like Napoleon. Similarly, a few of those
who knew Reilly during those years commented on his, Reilly's,
"Napoleonic" complex and ambitions. Indeed, during those crucial months in Moscow and Petrograd in the summer of 1918 he
appears to have believed that he would be the man who would
change the course of Russian history—which, by a stretch, meant,
as it turned out, change the course of world history. Reilly's failure that summer to engineer the overthrow of the Bolshevik
regime failed to stifle this ambition. During the following years
he mulled over his fate—and Russia's—and in 1924–1925 his ambition powerfully resurfaced when, in a last throw of the dice, he
reentered the Bolshevik maw to lay claim to the leadership of
the prospective counterrevolution. Reilly's drive to leave a personal mark on history was organically linked to his obsession
with overthrowing the hateful Bolshevik regime, which he regarded as subversive of, if not actually lethal to, Western Civilization. During that last, fatal journey from Paris to Finland
and across the Russian border, Reilly cast himself as the potential savior of Western Civilization, nothing less.

In this overarching passion of his last ten years Reilly was,
as we have seen, unsuccessful; he failed to remove the Bolsheviks from power—and assure himself a prominent place in his-

tory. Still, by virtue of his limited successes and dramatic failure that summer of 1918 he did assume a notable place in the annals of espionage. Had he lived long enough, he would surely have been overjoyed to witness Bolshevism's collapse at the end of the 1980s. But equally surely, he would have been much disheartened by what ensued, the emergence of the "Chekist" Russia of Vladimir Putin.

BIBLIOGRAPHICAL NOTE

TRACING THE LIFE of a spy is always difficult. He (or she, of course) operates in the shadows and most of what he does may never be consigned to paper. And if, somehow, some of his activities are documented, the paperwork will be held by intelligence agencies that deny access to researchers. Outside these agencies, the spy's colleagues and friends will usually keep mum or stay vague when interviewed and will generally leave our spy's life and doings memorably opaque. In the case of a spy who died a century ago, there is, of course, no one left to interview. And Sidney Reilly's life and career were such that his story is supremely turbid. He came from an empire that collapsed in chaos, where much of the paperwork has been lost, if it ever existed; and as an adult, he operated as a pieceworking part-timer, not as a long-standing permanent employee of a government agency that kept proper personnel and operational files. Hence, there is a paucity of accessible contemporaneous documentation about Sidney Reilly.

Nonetheless, some original documentation exists, and I have

been fortunate enough to tap most of it. MI5, the British security (or counterintelligence) service, kept a file (KV2/827) on Reilly, and it is open to the public. So are a number of relevant files in the United States National Archive. There is also accessible documentation on Reilly in the records of the Foreign and War Offices in Britain's National Archives (including in files FO 371/3319, 371/3326, 371/3332, 371/3340, 371/3348, 371/3350, 371/3961, 371/3962, 371/3963, 371/4021, 371/4024, and 371/11793; in J77/839/5502; and in WO 33/96, 372/16/193799, 372/2756, 32/5669, and 157/767). Fortunately, the Central Archives of Russia's Federal Security Service, the FSB, has opened to public scrutiny a key Cheka/OGPU file with Reilly material, 302330, vol. 37.

There are also a number of collections of private papers that contain material on Reilly. The most important are the papers of Robert Lockhart, including his diary for 1918, and of his son, Robin Bruce Lockhart, in the Hoover Library at Stanford University, California. Other useful collections that include material on Reilly are the papers of Brigadier-General Edward Spears in the Middle East Centre, St. Antony's College, Oxford, and the papers of General F. C. Poole, Military Archives, Kings College, London.

I have been fortunate in being a latecomer to the Sidney Reilly story. Thus I was able to benefit enormously from the spadework evidenced in previous biographies of the man. Among these, the most accurate and useful are Richard Spence's *Trust No One: The Secret World of Sidney Reilly* (2002) and Andrew Cook's *Ace of Spies: The True Story of Sidney Reilly* (2002). Both Spence and Cook enjoyed access, under a previous MI6 administration, to Reilly material in the agency's archive. Also useful have been Robin Bruce Lockhart's two volumes on the man, *Reilly: Ace of Spies* (1967) and *Reilly: The First Man* (1987). And there are a number of illuminating passages in Michael Kettle's *Sidney Reilly: The True Story* (1983). Taken together, these have afforded me a good chronological outline of the spy's life and adventures.

But an earlier volume has been of immense use as well, if only because it provided me with a "feel" for some of the personae involved, first and foremost Reilly himself—and this was *Britain's*

Master Spy: The Adventures of Sidney Reilly (1986, originally published by Harper & Row, 1932). The book is composed of two parts: a narrative ostensibly written by the last Mrs. Reilly, Pepita Bobadilla, which tells the story of Reilly's final two years, 1923–1925; and a narrative purportedly written by Reilly himself about his earlier life, focusing on his operations in Russia in 1918. The second narrative was apparently stitched together by Mrs. Reilly on the basis of notes and letters left by her husband as well as memories of what he or others had told her. Both parts were apparently ghostwritten, on the instructions of Bobadilla, by journalist Stuart Atherley six years after Reilly died.

A number of tangential memoirs have also been useful, chiefly George Alexander Hill's *Dreaded Hour* (1936) and *Go Spy the Land, Being the Adventures of IK8 of the British Secret Service* (1932). Hill spied with Reilly in Russia in 1918–1919, subsequently looked into Reilly's life (on orders of the head of SIS), and was a friend of Reilly's during the early twenties. Also of value have been Paul Dukes's *Red Dusk and the Morrow: Adventures and Investigations in Soviet Russia* (1922); Clare Sheridan's *Naked Truth* (1928); Maisie Ward's *Caryll Houselander* (1962); Alan Judd's *The Quest for C: Sir Mansfield Cumming and the Founding of the British Secret Service* (1999); and Deborah McDonald and Jeremy Dronfield's *A Very Dangerous Woman: The Lives, Loves, and Life of Russia's Most Seductive Spy* (2015).

In writing this biography I have been greatly served by a handful of volumes that provided historical background as regards Britain's intelligence agencies and their work on and in Russia during the period 1915–1925. The best books on the British intelligence services during those years are Christopher Andrew's *Her Majesty's Secret Service: The Making of the British Intelligence Community* (1985) and *Defend the Realm: The Authorized History of MI5* (2009), and Keith Jeffery's *The Secret History of MI6, 1909–1949* (2010). Also useful are Nigel West's *MI6: British Secret Intelligence Operations 1909–1945* (1983) and Michael Smith's *Six: A History of Britain's Secret Intelligence Service* (2010).

On the more general subject of the West and Russia during the relevant years I was aided by Laura Engelstein's *Russia in Flames:*

War, Revolution, Civil War 1914–1921 (2018); Evan Mawdsley's *The Russian Civil War* (2005); Gordon Brook-Shepherd's *Ironmaze: The Western Secret Services and the Bolsheviks* (1998); Harry Ferguson's *Operation Kronstadt: The True Story of Honor, Espionage, and the Rescue of Britain's Greatest Spy, the Man with a Hundred Faces* (2010); Giles Milton's *Russian Roulette: How British Spies Thwarted Lenin's Plot for Global Revolution* (2013); Robert Service's *Spies and Commissars: Bolshevik Russia and the West* (2011); Joshua Rubenstein's *Leon Trotsky: A Revolutionary's Life* (2011); and George F. Kennan's *Russia and the West under Lenin and Stalin* (1960). Some of these books devote extensive sections to Reilly's work in Russia in 1918–1925. Winston Churchill's portrait of Savinkov in *Great Contemporaries* (1932) was also useful.

For Reilly's early life before leaving Russia, I have relied mainly on the Spence and Cook biographies and on (often contradictory) statements by Reilly to his friends and lovers, especially Pepita Bobadilla. Steven Zipperstein's *The Jews of Odessa: A Cultural History, 1794–1881* (1991) and Charles King's *Odessa: Genius and Death in a City of Dreams* (2011) were useful in understanding where Reilly came from.

For Reilly's early connection to British intelligence I found useful Andrew Cook's *M: MI5's First Spymaster* (2006). On Reilly in Port Arthur, I have relied on what Reilly told various people, but also on Akashi Motojiro, *Rakka Ryūsui: Colonel Akashi's Report on His Secret Cooperation with the Russian Revolutionary Parties during the Russo-Japanese War* (1988), pp. 14 and 47–48; and Y. Tak Matsusaka, "Human Bullets, General Nogi, and the Myth of Port Arthur," in John W. Steinberg, Bruce W. Menning, David Schimmelpenninck van der Oye, David Wolff, and Shinju Yokote, eds., *The Russo-Japanese War in Global Perspective*, vol. 2: *World War Zero* (2005), pp. 184 and 186.

On Reilly in the United States during World War One, I have relied on the papers of the US Bureau of Investigation in the US National Archives and on MI5 reports on his activities. Most important are the USNA's "Investigative Records Relating to German Aliens ('Old German Files'), 1915–1920" (Record Group 65).

On Reilly in Moscow and Petrograd in 1918 (the so-called Lockhart Plot), of major use were two reports written by "participants" in the plot—George Hill's 28-page report from November 1918, "Report of Work Done in Russia to End of 1917 [*sic;* should be 1918]," UKNA FO 371/3350; and R. H. B. Lockhart's report of November 1918, "Secret and Confidential Memorandum on the Alleged 'Allied Conspiracy' in Russia," UKNA FO 371/3348. Robert H. B. Lockhart's *Memoirs of a British Agent: Being an Account of the Author's Early Life in Many Lands and of His Official Mission to Moscow in 1918* (1932) and the Reilly/Bobadilla concoction *Britain's Master Spy* (see above) also contain important material, as does Jonathan Schneer's *The Lockhart Plot: Love, Betrayal, Assassination, and Counter-Revolution in Lenin's Russia* (2020).

Two academic articles, John W. Long's "Searching for Sidney Reilly: The Lockhart Plot in Revolutionary Russia, 1918," *Europe-Asia Studies* 47, no. 7 (1995); and Richard Spence's "The Tragic Fate of Kalamatiano: America's Man in Moscow," *International Journal of Intelligence and Counterintelligence* 12, no. 3 (1999), also proved useful. Lastly, Roy Bainton's *Honoured by Strangers: The Life of Captain Francis Cromie CB DSO RN 1882–1918* (2002) provides useful detail.

For Reilly's (and Hill's) work in southern Russia, December 1918–March 1919, I have relied mainly on Reilly's and Hill's reports to be found in UKNA FO 371/3978, 371/3962, 371/3963, and 371/4021 and WO 157/766, 157/767. John Ainsworth, "Sidney Reilly's Reports from South Russia, December 1918–March 1919," *Europe-Asia Studies* 50, no. 8 (1998), also covers the period.

For Reilly's ejection from MI6 and his postwar years in business and espionage, I have relied mainly on Judd's *The Quest for C,* the Andrew volumes on British intelligence, and the Spence and Cook biographies.

For the end of the Reilly story and his capture and demise in Russia in 1925 I have relied mainly on the documents in the Reilly file in the FSB Archive and on Reilly/Bobadilla, *Britain's Master Spy.*

ACKNOWLEDGMENTS

I WOULD LIKE to thank Ulla Zueva for her help in researching in Russian archives and translating Russian texts.

I would also like to thank Anita Shapira for launching me on this project and supplying useful advice along the way.

Needless to say, I owe a debt to the archivists at the United States National Archives (College Park), the United Kingdom National Archives (London), and the FSB Archive (Moscow) for the help they afforded.

And, as usual, I thank my friend Jeff Abel for his help in getting all (I hope) my techno-computer ducks in a row in preparing the manuscript.

I would also like to thank my agent Georges Borchardt and the staff of Yale University Press for helping turn the manuscript into a book.

INDEX

Bugsy Siegel: The Dark Side of the American Dream,
    by Michael Shnayerson
Solomon: The Lure of Wisdom, by Steven Weitzman
Steven Spielberg: A Life in Films, by Molly Haskell
Alfred Stieglitz: Taking Pictures, Making Painters, by Phyllis Rose
Barbra Streisand: Redefining Beauty, Femininity, and Power,
    by Neal Gabler
Leon Trotsky: A Revolutionary's Life, by Joshua Rubenstein
Warner Bros: The Making of an American Movie Studio,
    by David Thomson
Elie Wiesel: Confronting the Silence, by Joseph Berger

FORTHCOMING TITLES INCLUDE:

Abraham, by Anthony Julius
Hannah Arendt, by Masha Gessen
Franz Boas, by Noga Arikha
Alfred Dreyfus, by Maurice Samuels
Anne Frank, by Ruth Franklin
Betty Friedan, by Rachel Shteir
George Gershwin, by Gary Giddins
Allen Ginsberg, by Ed Hirsch
Herod, by Martin Goodman
Jesus, by Jack Miles
Josephus, by Daniel Boyarin
Louis Kahn, by Gini Alhadeff
Mordecai Kaplan, by Jenna Weissman Joselit
Carole King, by Jane Eisner
Fiorello La Guardia, by Brenda Wineapple
Mahler, by Leon Botstein
Norman Mailer, by David Bromwich
Louis B. Mayer and Irving Thalberg, by Kenneth Turan